LAUGHING WITH THE HEAD BALL COACH

LAUGHING WITH THE HEAD BALL COACH

Humorous Tales of a Coaching Legend

Go 'Cocks

RICHARD SIKES

Richard Sikes

Old Bay Publishing
Huntsville, Alabama

Library of Congress Cataloging-in-Publication data is available.
ISBN: 0-9745854-1-6

Cover design by Hope Design
Page design by Mike Towle

Printed in the United States of America
1 2 3 4 5 6 —09 08 07 06

In Memory of Ellen Somerset and Ina Shockley

Contents

IV. Post Gainesville

ACKNOWLEDGMENTS

A LARGE DEBT IS OWED to *Huntsville Times* sports editor John Pruett, who first got me thinking about doing sports humor books. Steve Spurrier's boyhood friend and *Tennessean* sports columnist Joe Biddle was full of great stories and good advice for other sources of material. Steve Spurrier himself provided detail for a couple of stories, and his brother Graham Spurrier was very helpful. Spurrier's high school teammate Ken Lyon (a character in his own right) was a big help. Paul Gattis of the *Huntsville Times* put a lot of effort into finding an obscure story that I had not been able to locate. Last, but not least, a big debt is owed to my wife Nell, who has endured far too many sports anecdotes over the last thirty years.

Introduction: The Life of a Head Ball Coach

STEPHEN ORR SPURRIER WAS born April 20, 1945, in Miami Beach, Florida. He was the youngest of three children born to John Graham and Marjorie Spurrier. Spurrier's father was a Presbyterian minister, and he frequently moved his family in young Steve's early years. In 1947, the family moved from Miami to Athens, Tennessee.

Spurrier probably first became interested in football while living in Athens. Tennessee Wesleyan College, located in Athens, had strong junior-college teams during Steve's childhood days, and the youngster and his older brother Graham frequently watched the practices of the local college team. Steve was such a fixture at the practice sessions of Tennessee Wesleyan that he became the team mascot.

After his parents moved again, this time to Newport, Tennessee, young Spurrier had his first experience playing organized sports as a member of his elementary school's basketball team. His father had been a good athlete, and he encouraged his sons Graham and Steve to participate in sports. Reverend Spurrier was extremely competitive, and he once said that if winning was not important, then there would be no reason to keep score.

John Spurrier's sons inherited their dad's competitive nature, and Graham was a good high school athlete, while Steve was an outstanding basketball, football, and baseball player. Graham insists that part of the reason for his younger brother's development into such an outstanding athlete was because he always played sports against his dad and older brother. While in elementary school, Steve frequently scored twenty-five or thirty points in basketball games—which was about as many points as entire opposing teams could muster.

When he was about eight or nine years old, Steve got a football kicking tee for Christmas and practiced place kicking hour after hour. Although young Spurrier was a good natural athlete, his extremely competitive nature and hard work made him into a dominant force on the athletic field.

IN 1956 THE SPURRIERS moved from Newport to Johnson City, Tennessee, and young Steve began to blossom as a three-sport star. As an eleven-year-old, Spurrier scored forty of his team's forty-four points as his fifth-grade team beat a team from Morristown. Later, at Science Hill High School in Johnson City, Steve became an All-State player in baseball, basketball, and football. He was a dominating baseball pitcher, who was undefeated as a hurler in his last three years of high school. He led the baseball Hilltoppers to the Tennessee state championship in his last two years at Science Hill.

In basketball Steve was an outstanding shooter, and was ahead of his time with behind-the-back passes and between-the-legs dribbling. His flashy style of play and seemingly arrogant attitude on the basketball court made him the player that the opposing crowds loved to hate, a characteristic that has endured throughout his playing and coaching career. The enmity of opposing fans did not faze the cocky, young athlete, only making the competitive Spurrier more determined than ever to win.

As a football player young Spurrier experienced a growth spurt between his junior and senior years in high school, and during this period he changed from being a very good high school player to a great one.

Chicago Bears quarterback Bill Wade watched the Science Hill spring game before Spurrier's senior season, and he was extremely impressed with the potential of the young high school quarterback. Wade persuaded Coach Kermit Tipton to install more passing plays to utilize the talents of his budding signal caller. The change in the Hilltoppers' offense was a brilliant move, and the emphasis on more passing allowed Spurrier to earn high school All-American honors during his senior football season.

Of course, Spurrier's football exploits caught the attention of college recruiters throughout the nation, and they quickly beat a path to the door of the young phenom. As a youngster, young Steve grew up about a hundred miles from the college football hotbed of Knoxville, Tennessee, and he was a fan of the University of Tennessee Volunteers. He frequently attended Tennessee games with his family, and many observers assumed he would someday play college football for the home-state Vols.

Legendary Tennessee Coach Gen. Robert Neyland had built the Volunteers into a national powerhouse by emphasizing a sound kicking game, a stifling defense, and a conservative single-wing offense that relied on brute force and de-emphasized the passing game. The single-wing offense had no quarterback, and instead relied on a tailback, who had to be a bruising runner as well as able to throw the few passes that the power-oriented offense utilized. Obviously, this conservative offense was not a good fit for Spurrier's skills, and he quickly ruled the Volunteers out as a potential college choice.

Another college football program that attracted the attention of the hot-shot recruit from Johnson City was the University of Alabama. The Crimson Tide had been a national football power ever since they won the Rose Bowl in the 1920's, and were in the fifth year of the coaching tenure of the legendary Paul "Bear" Bryant. Bryant's 1961 team had won the national championship, and Bryant was already widely regarded as one of the country's best coaches. However, Alabama's quarterback in 1962 was a sophomore by the name of Joe Namath, and Namath figured to have a lock on the quarterback position for the next two years. Beyond that, 'Bama's quarterback of the future appeared to be highly regarded Steve Sloan, whose college eligibility would extend through 1965, which would be Spurrier's junior year in college.

Edwin Graves, whose brother was Florida coach Ray Graves, was a postmaster in Tennessee and he had seen Spurrier play high school ball. Edwin raved to his brother Ray about the potential of the prep star from Johnson City. At that time, Florida's program for years had had a reputation for bringing in talented athletes long on potential but short on dedication and the desire to win.

Ray Graves had played college ball for Neyland at UT, and he had begun to turn the Gator program around since being named coach at the Gainesville school in 1960. Also, from Spurrier's standpoint, the Gators' offensive coordinator was Pepper Rodgers, a former Georgia Tech star and renowned as a proponent of a wide open pro-style passing attack. Not only that, Spurrier was an avid golfer, and Florida's climate was conducive to playing golf year-round.

The Gators invited the young Tennessean to visit Gainesville so he could observe their 1963 spring game. Although Florida appeared to be well-stocked at the quarterback position, the brash college prospect told high school friend Joe Biddle that the

Gators did not have any quarterbacks better than him. After his visit to Gainesville, Spurrier announced his intention to play for the Gators.

PRIOR TO HIS MOVE to Gainesville to become the mentor of the Florida football program, Ray Graves had served as defensive coordinator for Bobby Dodd at Georgia Tech. Dodd had been very successful at Georgia Tech with a coaching style that emphasized that football should be fun for the coaches and players. That set Dodd, and subsequently Graves, apart from their brethren at most other college programs who viewed football with the solemnity of a military campaign.

Whereas other coaches emphasized hard-nosed blocking and real tackling during weekly practice sessions, Dodd was likely to have a short football practice session followed by a volleyball game for the coaches and players. When coaches who continually lost to Dodd called the Yellow Jackets lucky, Dodd retorted that "If you think you're lucky, you are." Florida's head coach Graves and offensive coordinator Pepper Rodgers (who played quarterback for Dodd at Georgia Tech) were strongly influenced by the laid-back Dodd style, and that influence was evident in Spurrier's coaching philosophy when he became a head coach.

Freshmen were not eligible to play on the varsity during Spurrier's playing days at Florida, which is why he did not become the starting quarterback until halfway through his sophomore season in 1964, which is when he led the Gators to a 7-3 record. The Gators also went 7-3 in Spurrier's junior season, which was highlighted by his late-game heroics in pulling out victories over arch-rivals Georgia and Florida State. Florida spotted Missouri a 20-0 lead in the 1966 Sugar Bowl, before a furious Spurrier-led fourth quarter rally pulled the Gators to within two points of the Tigers. While it was a loss for Florida, it was one more piece of evidence of how special a player he really was.

Florida began the 1966 season with six straight victories and was a strong favorite to make a 3-3 Auburn team their seventh victim. However, the over-confident Gators had all they could handle with the fired-up Tigers, who were tied with the Gators late in the game, with Florida facing fourth and thirteen on Auburn's twenty-four-yard line with only seconds left to play.

When Coach Graves tried to send in kicker Wayne Barfield to attempt what would be a game-winning forty-yard field goal, Spurrier decided that a forty-yard kick was out of Barfield's range; and the cocky quarterback himself said he would be the one to try the kick. It was a bold move, and the right one, as Spurrier connected on the kick to give Florida the victory. Spurrier had been one of the leading candidates for the Heisman Trophy before the Auburn game, and his game-winning field goal at game's end pretty much locked up his selection for the 1966 Heisman award.

A week later Florida's hopes for a perfect season and SEC championship were dashed by a 27-10 loss to arch-rival Georgia. The Bulldogs utilized a tremendous pass rush, sacking Spurrier numerous times and causing him to throw three interceptions. The Gators finished the regular season with an 8-2 record and closed it out with an Orange Bowl victory over Georgia Tech.

ALTHOUGH STEVE SPURRIER WAS the third player chosen in the 1967 NFL Draft, his nine-year career with the San Francisco 49ers offered nothing particularly memorable, with him serving primarily as a backup quarterback to John Brodie. Spurrier then played one year for the expansion Tampa Bay Buccaneers who became the first NFL team to post a "perfect" 0-14 record.

Laughing With the Head Ball Coach

After being released by the hapless Bucs after the 1976 season, Spurrier tried out for the Denver Broncos and the Miami Dolphins prior to the 1977 season, but he was released by both teams. After staying out of football in 1977, he began his coaching career in 1978 as offensive backfield coach on Doug Dickey's staff at Florida. When Dickey was fired after compiling a 4-7 record, new Florida coach Charlie Pell did not retain Spurrier, believing that Spurrier's low-stress approach to recruiting and coaching did not fit Pell's ideal of a successful assistant coach.

After being cut loose by Pell, Spurrier was offered a job as quarterback coach by Pepper Rodgers at Georgia Tech. Although Spurrier improved the Yellow Jackets' offensive performance in 1979, Rodgers was fired after a 4-6-1 record, and new Tech coach Bill Curry was not inclined to retain Spurrier because of his reputation of not being a hard worker. The decision not to retain Rodgers' quarterback coach would have long-term repercussions for Curry, however, as his Kentucky teams were pounded mercilessly by Spurrier's Florida teams in the 1990's.

After leaving the Yellow Jackets, Spurrier spent three years as offensive coordinator for the Duke Blue Devils; and then received his first head coaching job with the Tampa Bay Bandits of the now defunct

United States Football League. After compiling a 35-19 record in three years at Tampa Bay, Spurrier again became unemployed after the USFL folded following the 1985 season; and he spent the 1986 season out of football.

Spurrier began his highly successful career as a college head coach with Duke in 1987. Although Duke's football team had long been a doormat in the basketball-mad Atlantic Coast Conference, Spurrier coached the 1987 Blue Devils to a 5-6 record. To this day, that remains Spurrier's only losing season as a college head coach, and three of Duke's losses were by three points or less. Despite having most of his starters, including his quarterback and star receiver back in 1988, the ACC pigskin prognosticators picked Duke to come in dead last in the conference in Spurrier's second season. The "head ball coach" (as Spurrier referred to himself) surprised everyone by "coaching the Blue Devils up" to a 7-3-1 record.

The 1988 season included a memorable return to face his old home state Tennessee Volunteers before more than ninety thousand fans in Neyland Stadium. The brash young coach shocked the partisan UT crowd by storming to a 31-7 lead, and holding on for a startling 31-26 upset of the SEC football power. Spurrier's 1989 Duke team compiled an 8-4 record and won the school's first ACC championship in twenty-seven years.

DURING THE THREE YEARS THAT Spurrier spent in Durham reviving the Duke football program, the football team at his alma mater was in constant turmoil. When NCAA violations were uncovered in 1989, while the Gators were *already* on probation, Galen Hall was fired in the middle of the season and replaced by interim coach Gary Darnell. At the end of the 1989 season, Gator fans clamored for the return of their favorite son, and Spurrier returned to Gainesville to reinvigorate the Florida program in 1990.

The twelve years that Steve Spurrier spent as the coach of the Gators were the best in the history of the program. Florida had been a notable underachiever during most of the pre-Spurrier era, and had never won an SEC or a national championship. Although the "ball coach's" first Florida team had the SEC's best SEC record, the Gators were ineligible for the league championship because of NCAA sanctions that Spurrier had inherited from the Hall regime.

Spurrier's second Florida team claimed the school's first-ever league championship in 1991, and the Gators would go on to capture five more league titles under his leadership. The Gators won their only national championship in 1996. Spurrier dominated the SEC in the 1990's as no coach had dominated the league since Alabama's Bryant ruled the roost in the 1960's and 1970's.

Spurrier's Florida teams won at least ten games in nine of his twelve seasons coaching in Gainesville. His career record of 122-27-1 gave him a winning percentage of .817 in one of the toughest conferences in the nation. His SEC winning percentage at Florida of .861 (87-14) is the best in league history, and he and Bryant are the only SEC coaches to win four consecutive league titles.

In an unbelievable display of consistency, Spurrier's Gators teams were ranked in the national top-25 polls 202 out of a possible 203 weeks. After the league was divided into two divisions in 1992, Spurrier's Gators won the Eastern Division title seven times in ten years, and went on to win the SEC championship game five times.

STEVE SPURRIER'S FIRST GAME as head coach of the Florida Gators was a harbinger of things to come. The Gators scored quickly on a long drive the first time they had the ball, and they bombarded the over-matched Oklahoma State Cowboys, 50-7. For the next twelve years Spurrier's "fun 'n gun" offense would spread out the opposition's defense and run up huge numbers, both on the scoreboard and on the stat sheet. SEC football teams from the days of Tennessee's Neyland and Alabama's Bryant had relied on hard-nosed defenses and strong kicking games to grind out victories, but Spurrier's Gators would pummel opponents by previously unheard-of margins as his innovative, wide-open offenses would change the style of football played in the conference.

Before the Spurrier era, an SEC team that scored three or more touchdowns in a game was considered to have had an outstanding offensive performance. Spurrier changed all that, as the Gators' offensive genius frequently "hung fifty" on the opposition. The conventional "old school" coaches would ease up on an opponent having an off day, but Spurrier gleefully piled up as many yards and points as he could.

Where conventional coaches would run out the clock rather than score another touchdown on an out-manned foe, Spurrier would try long passes and trick plays late in games in which the Gators already had huge leads. While other coaches would go to great lengths not to say anything negative about an opponent to get them riled up before a game, the "Evil Genius" (as Georgia fans called him) took great delight in poking fun at the opposition. When his Gators dominated the Tennessee Volunteers in the mid-1990's and annually relegated UT to the less desirable Citrus Bowl, Spurrier regaled Gator boosters with his observation that it was not possible to spell Citrus Bowl without a "UT." The Citrus Bowl was played in Orlando, Florida, and Spurrier playfully declared Orlando the "winter home of the Tennessee Volunteers."

While most other football coaches were a model of stoicism on the sideline during a game, "the Evil Genius" was a whirling dervish on the Gator sideline. Bear Bryant had been a model of decorum and sartorial splendor, wearing his trademark hound's tooth hat as he coached his Alabama teams, but Spurrier was most comfortable in a golf shirt and his trademark visor while "coaching up" the Gators.

If things did not go well on a given play, the "head ball coach" was likely to give the visor a heave and was also prone to give a player (especially a quarterback) some up close and personal instruction when he thought it was required during a game.

Besides visor tossing, other sideline routines included headphone jerking, extreme grimacing, and running his hands through his hair. As Spurrier's success at Florida continued and his antics drew more attention, he became the man that opponents most loved to hate. Gator-haters loved to see a flying visor because they knew that something had upset "Darth Visor." Many of the highly ranked Gators' games were televised, and the TV crews always devoted one camera to the head Gator's sideline antics.

SOUTHEASTERN FOOTBALL FANS HAD never seen such a brash and cocky coach, let alone one who could back up his barbs so consistently. He infuriated opposing fans by telling them how badly the Gators were going to beat their teams, and then doing exactly what he said. During Spurrier's twelve-year tenure at Florida, the Gators beat their arch-rivals, the Georgia Bulldogs, an amazing eleven times. Vince Dooley, Georgia's athletic director during that time, summed up the feeling of most football fans whose teams had been hammered by Spurrier-led Gator teams when he said, "He's got a way of irritating fans."

Besides having the best record in the SEC while at Florida, Spurrier was also the league's dominant personality. He was a master at entertaining the fans and the media, while frosting the opposition. He had the ability to unite SEC fans in support of whoever was playing the Gators.

Some considered him to be an offensive genius; others just considered him offensive. Sports memorabilia shops throughout the South sold T-shirts proclaiming, "Will Rogers Never Met Steve Spurrier." When the Gators were doing well (they usually were) during a game, a sly smirk and arrogant air were his sideline trademark. A former teammate said, "I've never seen so many people hate a guy in my life. But he doesn't care."

AFTER LEADING FLORIDA THROUGH the twelve most productive years in their football history, Spurrier abruptly resigned after the 2001 season. He had long wanted to give professional football another shot, and he opted to sign a lucrative contract to coach the Washington Redskins. However, his stint with the Redskins did not go as well as his previous pro-coaching job with the Tampa Bay Bandits, and he resigned after two seasons during which his Redskins won only twelve games while losing twenty.

After leaving the Redskins, Spurrier stayed out of football for a year—obviously, one-year sabbaticals were nothing new to Spurrier—before returning to the SEC as head coach of the University of South Carolina Gamecocks in 2005. After his disappointing NFL experience, Spurrier was more subdued than usual upon his return to college ball. He promised to keep future jokes at the expense of the opposition to himself, and that he would concentrate on winning games for the lowly Gamecocks.

Prior to Spurrier's arrival at USC, the Gamecocks had won one conference championship and three bowl games in 111 years of playing football. During his introductory press conference in Columbia, the new "ball coach" observed that "they haven't done much here. That doesn't mean it can't change."

Despite losing their first three SEC games in 2005, South Carolina rebounded to finish the season with a 7-5 record that included a 38-31 loss to Missouri in the Independence Bowl (two of the other four losses were by two and four points to Georgia and Clemson, respectively). Although the Gamecocks were not expected to do well in Steve Spurrier's first year at the helm, they defeated both traditional national power Tennessee as well as Spurrier's alma mater, the Florida Gators, who had just hired Urban Meyer while snubbing the available Spurrier in the process. South Carolina has had two other coaches who had previously won national titles (Paul Dietzel and Lou Holtz) who did not do well with the Gamecocks, and it remains to be seen if Spurrier can replicate his previous success at Duke and Florida with the Gamecocks.

LAUGHING WITH THE HEAD BALL COACH

I.
THE EARLY
YEARS

I
Alone Behind
Enemy Lines

ALTHOUGH STEVE SPURRIER WOULD go on to become an All-American college football player, many people who followed his high school athletic career considered basketball to be his best sport. He was capable of scoring thirty to forty points per game, and played the game with a flair that was uncommon in the late fifties and early sixties. With his flashy behind-the-back passing and between-the-legs dribbling, the cocky youngster from Johnson City became the player that opposing crowds loved to hate.

Dobyns-Bennett High School in Kingsport, Tennessee, had a rich basketball tradition, and their fans did not relish being upstaged by a brat from Spurrier's Science Hill Hilltoppers. After Spurrier put

1

on a great performance to lead the Hilltoppers to a victory over Dobyns-Bennett in Kingsport and enraged the local fans with his brash antics, he became preoccupied talking to the media in the locker room after the game.

While Spurrier talked and talked, his teammates showered and dressed for the return trip to Johnson City. They then boarded the team bus, although the Hilltoppers' coach did not realize that his star player was not on the bus as it left Kingsport. When the cocky Spurrier emerged from the shower, he realized that his teammates had already departed for Johnson City, and he concluded that he did not have a lot of admirers in Kingsport who would offer him a ride home. Fortunately for young Spurrier, an assistant coach at Dobyns-Bennett had coached him in junior high school in Johnson City, and he offered the young athlete a ride home.

2
Two-for-One Recruiting

As a high school All-American quarterback at Science Hill High School in Johnson City, Tennessee, Steve Spurrier was heavily recruited by college teams throughout the country. Paul "Bear" Bryant invited the prospect to Tuscaloosa, but Spurrier was not interested in signing with the Crimson Tide because Alabama was already blessed with an abundance of quarterback talent.

Jack Green, the coach of traditional SEC patsy Vanderbilt, decided to take an innovative approach to recruiting the heralded signal caller. Spurrier's favorite receiver in high school, Jimmy Sanders, was not pursued by other major colleges because, at only five foot eight and 150 pounds, he was not considered

Vanderbilt invited the high school teammates to Nashville, and impressed them with a tour of the Governor's Mansion and a fine meal at an upscale restaurant.

big enough to play college ball. The Commodores believed that if they could entice Sanders to accept a scholarship, they could use that angle to lure Spurrier to follow Sanders, his favorite receiver, to Nashville. Vanderbilt invited the high school teammates to Nashville, and impressed them with a tour of the Governor's Mansion and a fine meal at an upscale restaurant. After the meal, Sanders was offered an athletic scholarship, and the savvy receiver (he later became a very successful attorney) quickly accepted the offer.

The Vanderbilt coaches then informed Spurrier that his teammate had signed with the Commodores, and offered him a scholarship that would allow him to continue throwing passes to his favorite high school receiver. The quarterback informed the Vandy coaches that he had been invited to Gainesville to watch the Florida spring game, and he did not want to make a decision about his choice of colleges until he had made the Florida visit.

The Commodores coaching staff knew that Florida had a talented corps of signal callers, and they assumed that Spurrier would cast his lot with

Vanderbilt after seeing the amount of competition he would be facing in Gainesville. After Spurrier returned from his trip to Florida, Coach Green called him and asked him how the trip to the Sunshine State had gone. The young quarterback said the weather had been great, and that he had thoroughly enjoyed a round of golf on the university's golf course. The Vandy coach then decided to play his trump card by asking Spurrier if he had observed how talented the Gators were at the quarterback position. By then Spurrier had already decided to cast his lot with the Gators, and the brash high schooler told Coach Green that he had not seen any quarterbacks "that I couldn't beat" in Gainesville.

3

The Next Great Quarterback?

AFTER STEVE SPURRIER LEFT his hometown of Johnson City, Tennessee, to attend the University of Florida, he still kept in touch with his high school pals, and would frequently invite them to come to Gainesville to see him play for the Gators. Close high school friend Joe Biddle, who would later become a Tennessean sports columnist on occasion covering Spurrier, received numerous invitations to watch his old high school crony perform at Florida Field.

Biddle was accompanied on many of the trips to the Sunshine State by another Spurrier confidante from Johnson City, Gary Wayne Fisher. These trips from the hills of Tennessee to Florida were 570 miles each way, and they were an exhausting undertaking in the days before the interstate highway system had been completed.

However, when the exhausted Tennesseans arrived in Gainesville, they were provided "lavish" accommodations that included the privilege of sleeping on the floor in Spurrier's dormitory room that he shared with roommate Bill Carr, an All-American center for the Gators.

Besides the posh sleeping arrangements, Spurrier continued in his role of being the perfect host by providing his old buddies tickets to the game. Fisher, who was five foot seven and approximately 110 pounds, would be given a student ticket and Carr's student identification. Apparently, the ushers checking student ID's did not closely monitor their use since "the Fish" was not exactly a dead ringer for Carr, who stood six-four and weighed 230.

Spurrier made sure his out-of-town guests received proper nourishment by sneaking them into the dining area where the athletes ate. In order to insure that his friend "the Fish" was treated with the utmost respect at the athlete's training table, Spurrier advised the other athletes and dining hall staff that the strapping 110-pounder was the hottest quarterback prospect to come out of Tennessee since Steve himself had enrolled at Florida. Spurrier informed everyone that although "the Fish" was small in stature, he was as quick as greased lightning and had an arm like a rocket. To complete the charade, Spurrier and "Fish the phenom" would stay on top of their games by throwing imaginary passes to each other as they caroused around the dining hall.

4

Steve the Scholar

THROUGHOUT HIS YEARS IN elementary, junior high, and high school, Spurrier definitely put more emphasis on athletics than he did on academics. Paul Finebaum, a popular radio sports talk show host in Alabama, said that the only time that Spurrier did not run up the score was when he took the SAT.

Although he was a bright guy, Spurrier was classified as being an average student—at best. During the summer of 1966, preceding his senior season at the University of Florida, he took one course in summer school. The course, which was called Human Growth and Development, was a physical education class that would not have qualified as a pre-requisite for a degree in astro-physics. It was common knowledge at Florida that the professor who taught the course favored football players, and Spurrier was not greatly surprised when he received an A at the end of the summer session.

At that time, the academic All-American team was selected based on grades from the last semester completed before the academic honors team was picked. There were no restrictions on the type of courses taken or the number of credit hours earned. Norm Carlson, Florida's sports information director, was aware of the selection criteria for the academic All-American team, and he nominated the Gators' star, who was selected as first-team academic All-American quarterback.

"Well, I don't know how that happened. I only took one course. It was in football. It was four hours credit, and the guy favored football players."

Carlson trumpeted the Florida's star selection to the academic honor team with great fanfare, and told the quarterback that when his selection to the team was announced he should say something to the effect that it was a great honor to be selected. However, when Spurrier was asked about his selection by the Florida beat writer for the *Miami Herald*, he answered in the brutally honest manner that would later become a Spurrier trademark. He told the Miami reporter, "Well, I don't know how that happened. I only took one course. It was in football. It was four hours credit, and the guy favored football players; maybe that's why he's no longer employed at the PE school."

5
Right Here on Our Stage

For twenty-three years between 1948 and 1971, Ed Sullivan's weekly television variety show ruled the Sunday night airwaves. The performers on his show ran the gamut from opera singers, ballet dancers, and comedians, to jugglers, puppets, and trained animal acts. Sullivan was a keen judge of talent, and his show featured acts that the American public wanted to see.

Being featured on the Sullivan show signified that an entertainer had "arrived." In the 1950's Sullivan introduced a relatively unknown singer from Memphis named Elvis Presley to his vast audience, and in the 1960's he presented four musicians from

Liverpool, England, known collectively as the Beatles to the USA.

Besides being a great talent scout, Sullivan was known for two other features: a wooden delivery of any announcement that he made on the show, and a tremendous talent for botching the introduction of guests on the telecast. In describing Sullivan's style as an emcee, one television critic said that a first-time viewer of his show might think that the regular master of ceremonies had not shown up, and the night security guard had been given the script, changed into a suit, and hustled onto the stage to introduce the acts. He had once introduced impressionist Rich Little by saying, "Let's hear it for this fine young Canadian comic, Buddy Rich." (Buddy Rich was a well-known drummer at the time). When introducing Metropolitan opera star Robert Merrill he said, "I'd like to *prevent* Robert Merrill."

The All-American football team was presented to the nation each fall through an appearance on Sullivan's television show. Obviously, Steve Spurrier was the quarterback on the 1966 team after his Heisman Trophy season that year. Although Sullivan was a great talent scout, he was not an avid college football fan, and his introduction of the 1966

All-American team only added to the tales of his botched introductions. First, the hapless TV host introduced Syracuse running back Floyd Little as Spurrier. Then, after being told of the gaffe by the show's producer, Sullivan brought Spurrier back onto the stage and introduced him as "Steve Spurrier of the University of Miami.

II.
PRELUDE TO GREATNESS

6
Coach, Your Son Stinks

COACH JOHN MCKAY HAD an enviable record while coaching the University of Southern California. During McKay's sixteen years there, the Trojans won four national championships, posted three unbeaten seasons, won the Pacific Eight Conference championship nine times, and he was the winningest coach in USC history with a record of 127-40-8.

McKay's initial foray into professional football, however, was not quite as successful as his college career. Part of the reason for his early lack of success in the professional ranks was due to coaching the expansion Tampa Bay Buccaneers in an era when expansion teams had rosters filled with players that the other NFL teams did not want. One of those "unwanted" players was Steve Spurrier, who had had a less-than-distinguished career as backup quarterback to John Brodie of the San Francisco 49ers. However, one of Spurrier's better performances for the Forty-Niners had been a game against the Los Angeles Rams that McKay had attended in Los Angeles. So when Spurrier became available in the NFL expansion draft, the coach was interested in bringing Spurrier back to the state where he had won the Heisman Trophy ten years earlier.

Spurrier and McKay did not get along in Tampa. For one thing the coach did not think his quarterback was serious enough about helping him build a team for the future. McKay expected his veteran signal caller to act as a mentor to his younger Bucs teammates, but the laid-back Spurrier was more interested in getting to the golf course after practice than sticking around to help the younger players. In team meetings McKay expected his quarterback to be a rah-rah team leader, but Spurrier was pretty much indifferent to the proceedings.

The single biggest point of contention between the coach and the quarterback was that the coach's favorite pass receiver on the team happened to be the quarterback's least favorite receiver—J. K. McKay, the coach's son. Although J. K. had been a standout receiver on two of his father's national championship teams at USC and the Most Valuable Player in the 1975 Rose Bowl, he was a mediocre NFL player at best.

However, the legendary coach still envisioned his son as a fine receiver, and one day during pre-season practice in 1976 he asked Spurrier why he wasn't throwing more passes to the young McKay. Brutal honesty had always been one of Spurrier's characteristics, and he told Coach McKay point blank, "Well, he's the worst receiver on the squad, Coach."

Brutal honesty had always been one of Spurrier's characteristics.

7

Right Here in Tampa

WHILE JOHN MCKAY HAD been coach at Southern Cal, leaving there after the 1975 season to become coach of the NFL's expansion team based in Tampa, his coaching philosophy had emphasized a strong running game and a rock-ribbed defense.

His conservative bent inclined him to pick massive defensive end Lee Roy Selmon of the University of Oklahoma as his first pick in the 1976 NFL Draft. McKay's plan was to emphasize defense to keep the games close, and hope that the offense could score enough points to eke out a few victories. Rather than risk a high draft choice on a collegiate quarterback to lead the offense, the Bucs decided to utilize Spurrier and took him from San

Francisco in the expansion draft. Having played his college ball in not-too-distant Gainesville, the Bucs figured the former Heisman winner would also help fill the stadium.

Although Spurrier did play considerably more in his only NFL season for the Buccaneers than he had played for San Francisco, the 1976 season was not a complete artistic success. The Bucs provided a glimmer of hope for their fans when they won their pre-season game against the Atlanta Falcons, 17-3. However, Bucs fans were quickly brought back to the real world when the regular season began with a 20-0 shutout loss to the Houston Oilers. This performance proved to be an accurate harbinger of things to come as the Tampa Bay franchise became the first (and only) team in NFL history to compile a "perfect" 0-14 record. As loss despairingly followed loss, sportswriters asked McKay what he thought of the team's "execution," and the coach quipped that he was all for it.

During a pep talk after a practice session in that disastrous inaugural season, McKay reminded the Bucs of the old football cliché that most games are won and lost in the trenches, where good blocking and tackling were essential to success on the scoreboard. As the frustrated coach attempted to fire up his troops, he noticed offensive lineman Howard Fest (whose efforts would be vital to achieving success in the trenches) had nodded off to sleep. When McKay called Fest's name, it awakened the hulking lineman, and the coach asked him, "Where are most games lost"? The startled lineman earnestly replied "Coach, most games are lost right here in Tampa."

8
Knifing the Mack

COACH MACK BROWN ASCENDED to the top of the college football world in 2005, when his Texas Longhorns won the national championship by defeating the USC Trojans in the 2006 Rose Bowl. Despite his success, Brown's early years as a head coach gave little indication that he was necessarily traveling a path that would eventually lead to a national championship.

One of Brown's early coaching jobs was at the University of North Carolina, and many of his trials and tribulations in Chapel Hill were attributable to another rising star in the coaching world. While Brown was serving his apprenticeship at UNC, Steve Spurrier was learning how to be "a head ball coach" at the Tar Heels' arch rivals –the Duke Blue Devils. Although Brown would later enjoy considerable success during his ten years at UNC, his first two seasons at Chapel Hill ended with identical 1-10 records in both 1988 and 1989.

In light of Brown's early struggles at UNC and his endless stream of "coach-speak" cliches, Spurrier facetiously called him "Mr. Football." While Mack Brown was struggling at UNC, his brother Watson Brown was also having very limited success as head coach at the graveyard of SEC coaches, Vanderbilt. The impish Spurrier could not resist the temptation to label the duo "The Lose Brothers."

As the Tar Heels limped into the last game of Brown's second year with a 1-9 record, they were considerable underdogs to Spurrier's Blue Devils, who with a victory would win a share of their first Atlantic Coast Conference championship in twenty-seven years.

Spurrier had installed a high-octane offense for the Blue Devils, and they came into the season finale averaging thirty-two points per game. He had revived a moribund Duke football team that had won only twenty-nine games in the eight years before his arrival, and he won five games in 1987;

seven games in 1988; and had already compiled seven victories as the Blue Devils headed into their season finale at North Carolina.

To add further insult to injury, Spurrier after the game had the victorious Blue Devils pose for a picture in front of the UNC scoreboard.

The showdown in the big rivalry proved to be a huge mismatch, as Duke quarterback Dave Brown set an all-time school passing record with 479 yards in leading the Blue Devils to a humiliating 41-0 defeat of the Tar Heels. In a precursor of things to come for later Spurrier opponents, the Duke coach ordered up a last-minute touchdown to increase the Blue Devils' lead from thirty-four points to the final forty-one.

To add further insult to injury, Spurrier after the game had the victorious Blue Devils pose for a picture in front of the UNC scoreboard, which still displayed the 41-0 final score. When an enraged Brown complained to sportswriters about Spurrier's outlandish conduct, the cocky Duke coach said that he could not understand why Brown was so mad since, "I've won more games on that field than he has."

9
Low-Stress Recruiting

WHEN STEVE SPURRIER WAS taken in the 1976 NFL expansion draft by the Tampa Bay Buccaneers, the Bucs thought that the savvy veteran would help develop their younger players. However, Spurrier seemed to be more interested in improving his golf game than he was in tutoring the young Tampa Bay players. Rather than sticking around after practice to help the team's neophytes, the veteran quarterback would head for the nearest golf course. Spurrier's attitude irritated Bucs' coach John McKay, and the signal caller was put on waivers at the end of the disastrous 1976 season in which Tampa Bay became the first professional football team to go 0-14.

After staying out of football in 1977, Spurrier was hired as backfield coach by Florida coach Doug Dickey and charged with the task of taking the Gators out of the outdated wishbone offense and installing a wide-open pro-style attack. When the Gators stumbled to a 4-7 record in 1978, Dickey (who had been Florida's quarterback in the 1950's) was fired and replaced by Clemson coach Charlie Pell. As a player, Pell had been one of the undersized, quick linemen that Alabama Coach Paul "Bear" Bryant had used to dominate the SEC in the early 1960's. What Pell lacked in size and talent was more than compensated for by an aggressive personality and a strong work ethic. The new Gator coach had heard some of the rumors about Spurrier's less-than-intense coaching style, but still decided to interview the former Heisman Trophy winner to evaluate whether Spurrier would be a good fit on his coaching staff.

During Pell's interview with Spurrier, the head coach asked the assistant how recruiting was coming along. Each assistant coach is assigned an area to recruit, and talent-rich Jacksonville was in Spurrier's region. Recruiting in Jacksonville after the 1978 season was dominated by efforts to secure the services of a high school All-American running back from Wolfson High School named John L. Williams, and

Pell asked Spurrier how the Gators' recruitment of Williams was going. The assistant told the hyper head coach "I think we're in pretty good with him."

Recruiting is the life-blood of a big time college sports program, necessary to insure a steady stream of talent for the school, and the intense Pell expected an assistant to almost move into the house with a high-profile recruit such as Williams. When the coach was not physically with the prospect, he should telephone him constantly so that the university could respond to any whim that the youngster might have.

When the intense Pell heard Spurrier's assessment that, "I think we're in pretty good with him," he followed up by asking, "Who in the family are you working on to try to get him to Florida, and how many times have you been in his home?" The laid-back Spurrier answered that he hadn't actually been up to visit the Williams family, but he had seen the coveted prospect play in one high school game. Spurrier's *laissez faire* recruiting of Williams convinced Pell that the rumors about the assistant's work ethic were accurate, and Spurrier, who had been released by three professional football teams in 1977, was again unemployed.

10
The One That Got Away

FOR MANY YEARS LSU football fans had been long suffering since Paul Dietzel's 1958 team surprised almost everyone by winning the national championship. After Dietzel left LSU to coach Army following the 1961 season, the performances of the Bengal Tigers have ranged from good to mediocre to pathetic, but they never won another national championship until early in the twenty-first century.

After Bill Arnsparger retired as the Tigers' head coach following the 1986 season, a panel of Louisiana politicians and important alumni who constituted the LSU board of supervisors set about to find a replacement for Arnsparger. At the time Steve Spurrier was unemployed since his previous employer, the Tampa

Bay Bandits, were members of the recently disbanded United States Football League.

The board of supervisors dutifully compiled a list of fifteen candidates whom they deemed worthy of an interview with the august body. Spurrier's name was one of the fifteen, but his performance during his first interview apparently did not impress the Bayou state politicos who didn't deem him worthy of a follow-up session. One Louisiana sportswriter compared the politicians' failure to hire Spurrier to the Boston Red Sox' ill-fated decision to sell a promising young pitcher named Babe Ruth to the New York Yankees in 1920.

After being rebuffed by the Tigers, Spurrier was hired to rebuild a Duke University football program that had been floundering since the early 1960's. By the end of Spurrier's third year at Duke, his Blue Devils were co-champions of the Atlantic Coast Conference. After returning to the Florida Gators in 1990, he transformed his alma mater's perennial under-achieving football team into a national power-house that won six SEC championships and one national title. Meanwhile, the three coaches who coached LSU for the remainder of the twentieth century compiled a record of 82-74-3, and all three were fired at the end of their tenures in Baton Rouge.

III.
BACK IN
GAINESVILLE

11
Settling an Old Score

A FTER SPURRIER WAS RELEASED as a player by the
Tampa Bay Buccaneers at the end of the 1976
NFL season, he stayed out of football for one year
before taking a job as the quarterback coach for Doug
Dickey at his alma mater, the University of Florida.
Dickey was fired after a lackluster 4-7 season in 1978,
and Spurrier was not retained on the staff of new
Gators coach Charlie Pell.

After leaving Florida, Spurrier was offered a job
as the quarterback coach under Pepper Rodgers at
Georgia Tech. Rodgers had been offensive coordinator at Florida during Spurrier's playing career in
Gainesville, and he knew that his old quarterback

was a fierce competitor and had a very innovative approach to coaching offensive football.

Spurrier did an outstanding job in developing Tech's Mike Kelly into a first-rate college quarterback, and Kelly became the first quarterback in school history to pass for more than two thousand yards in a season. However, despite the high-powered offense, Tech's record in 1979 was only 4-6-1, and Rodgers was fired at the end of the season. Rodgers's replacement was former Tech All-American center Bill Curry, who decided not to keep Spurrier on his staff. Spurrier claimed that Curry simply did not offer him a job, but Curry claimed that Spurrier left Atlanta before the new head coach could interview him.

After being waived out of the NFL and fired by two college teams in two years, Spurrier never forgot how unforgiving the life of a football coach was, and he developed a deep fear of failure.

After being waived out of the NFL and fired by two college teams in two years, Spurrier never forgot how unforgiving the life of a football coach was, and he developed a deep fear of failure. He also never forgot that Curry had declined the opportunity to keep him on his coaching staff at Georgia Tech. Years later Spurrier said, "I'll show those people they were wrong, the ones that didn't keep me as a coach. We all like to prove people wrong who say we're no good." Over the next seventeen years Spurrier-coached teams would play against Curry's teams ten times, and Spurrier's teams won all ten of those games.

After not being retained on Curry's Georgia Tech staff, Spurrier was hired to be Duke's offensive coordinator by Red Wilson in 1980. During the three years that followed, Spurrier turned an anemic Duke offense into a powerhouse. During that time the Blue Devils defeated the Yellow Jackets by an average of twelve points per game, and Spurrier's 1981 and 1982 offenses both rang up thirty-eight points on the Curry-led Ramblin' Wreck.

After the 1986 season Curry left Georgia Tech to become head coach at the University of Alabama. Despite compiling a successful record with the Crimson Tide, Curry was never accepted by Alabama fans, mainly because he had committed the unpardonable sin of having no previous connection to legendary Alabama coach Paul "Bear" Bryant, and Curry left Tuscaloosa to coach the Kentucky Wildcats after the 1989 season. It was not a happy coincidence for Curry that his first year in Lexington was also Spurrier's first year as head coach at Florida. Spurrier would be the head coach of the Gators for all seven of the seasons that Curry led the Wildcats.

The first Florida/Kentucky showdown between Spurrier and Curry would be indicative of the six that would follow. In that 1990 game the Gators pounded the Wildcats 47-15 in Gainesville. The 1991 and 1993 games in Lexington were the only ones in which the Gators' margin of victory was less than ten points. In the 1993 game Florida needed a last-second touchdown pass to pull out a 24-20 victory. After the 1993 scare, "the head ball coach" no longer took the Wildcats lightly, and the 1994 match in "the Swamp" was a 73-7 laugher. The Wildcats did only slightly better in 1995 in Lexington as they were hammered 43-7.

Spurrier saved his best performance against a Curry-coached team for Curry's last visit to "the Swamp" in 1996. That game featured a 65-0 shutout in which the Kentucky offense was held to a meager sixty-seven yards of total offense, and the final score produced the highest-scoring shutout in the history of Florida football. The Wildcats' offense went three plays and out on their first seven possessions, and achieved only five first downs.

The Gators' seventy-eight-yard touchdown drive to open the game consumed only sixty-three seconds of the first quarter and exceeded Kentucky's output for the entire afternoon. After Florida's Jacquez Green returned two consecutive punts for touchdowns, Gator quarterback Danny Wuerffel joked that the offense would get rusty unless they told Green to start making fair catches.

12
The Tweaking
of the Orange

ALTHOUGH STEVE SPURRIER WAS born in Miami, Florida, his parents moved to east Tennessee when he was two years old, and he grew up in the heart of Big Orange country. As a youngster his favorite team was the local Tennessee Volunteers, and his family attended many UT games in Knoxville during his formative years.

However, when young Spurrier was a highly recruited high school quarterback at Johnson City's Science Hill High School, the Volunteers still used an out-dated single-wing offense that would not fully utilize Spurrier's passing ability, and he had little interest in playing for the Vols. He was briefly recruited by SEC and national powerhouse

Alabama, but the Crimson Tide had quarterbacks Joe Namath and Steve Sloan on the roster, and Spurrier decided to look elsewhere.

Edwin Graves, the brother of Florida coach Ray Graves, lived in Knoxville, and he told his brother that he should recruit the talented high school quarterback from Johnson City. The Gators' offensive coordinator was Pepper Rodgers, who had played for Bobby Dodd at Georgia Tech, and Rodgers' wide-open passing game would allow the young Spurrier to utilize his passing and play-calling talents. Spurrier decided to cast his lot with Florida, and he had an outstanding career with the Gators, which culminated with his winning the Heisman Trophy in his senior season in 1966.

Spurrier had an undistinguished career in professional football with the San Francisco 49ers and the Tampa Bay Buccaneers. After leaving the NFL after the 1976 season, his path did not cross that of the Volunteers until 1988, which was his second year as a college head coach with the Duke Blue Devils. Before Spurrier became head coach at Duke in 1987, the Blue Devils had won twenty-nine games in the previous eight years and had been a perennial doormat in the basketball-crazy Atlantic Coast Conference since the mid-1960's.

Laughing With the Head Ball Coach

Duke posted an amazing (for them) five victories in Spurrier's first season, and four of the losses were by a touchdown or less. Despite this promising start and the fact that "the head ball coach" had most of his starters returning in 1988, the football prognosticators picked the Blue Devils to finish last in the ACC in the coach's second year. After Duke opened the 1988 season with a victory over Northwestern, they went into Tennessee's Neyland Stadium to face traditional SEC and national football powerhouse Tennessee.

At first glance the game appeared to be a classic mismatch with the Volunteers a perennial force to be reckoned with in the football-dominated SEC, and Duke, the weak sister in the ACC. However, Spurrier had his team ready to play, and they stunned the home team by surging to a 28-0 halftime lead. They still led by 31-7 in the third quarter, and hung on for a 31-26 victory before a stunned crowd that exceeded ninety thousand (mostly UT) fans. Although Tennessee exacted a measure of revenge with a 28-6 victory over Duke in 1989, the stunning 1988 defeat by the Blue Devils would serve as fair warning to UT partisans for future encounters with the brash, cocky coach who had grown up only one hundred miles from Knoxville.

During Spurrier's first two years as coach of the Florida Gators, he split two games with the Johnny Majors-coached Volunteers. Once Spurrier got into a shouting match with Majors at a coaches' meeting in Hawaii. That was when the Gators coach made an incendiary remark about Majors's inability to beat border-state rival Alabama in the late 1980's and early 1990's. When Majors was asked about the confrontation, the coach of the Volunteers said, "He will express himself, I'll leave it at that." Then, in a classic understatement Majors said, "He's not bashful about talking about himself or his team."

In the 1992 Tennessee-Florida game, Majors was not able to coach the Vols because of heart surgery, and interim coach Phillip Fulmer led Tennessee to a 31-14 victory in Knoxville. It was the first year of the Southeastern Conference being divided into eastern and western divisions, and for the first ten years of divisional play the Tennessee-Florida winner would have an inside track to represent the eastern division in the conference championship game.

Florida or Tennessee won the eastern division title in each of the first ten years of divisional play, with Florida winning seven times while Tennessee was victorious the other three. Spurrier also won seven of his ten games versus Fulmer while coaching

Florida, and defeated him in his first year back in the SEC (2005) as coach at South Carolina.

In addition to the repeated beatings that Spurrier administered to Tennessee in this period, he also infuriated Volunteer fans with his sarcastic remarks about their team. Every year in that span the team that won the SEC championship won the home team berth in the Sugar Bowl. The runner-up in the eastern division was typically relegated to playing in the less prestigious Citrus Bowl.

After several Gator victories had sent the Volunteers to the Citrus Bowl, Spurrier regaled Gator booster clubs with his observation that it was impossible to spell "Citrus Bowl" without a "UT." During the 1996 off-season, he said that they had just hung up a new sign at the Citrus Bowl in Orlando proclaiming that city "the winter home of the Tennessee Volunteers." He also informed the Florida faithful that, "Yeah, that stadium up in Knoxville sure was loud. Then the game started."

After the 1996 game in Knoxville, which Florida won 35-29, Spurrier enraged UT fans by purporting to go through the list of Volunteer goals for the season. The first goal of winning the national championship had been thwarted by the loss to the Gators. The second goal of winning the conference championship was also unachievable after the Florida victory. The supposed third goal was Tennessee state champions, but an early season upset loss to the University of Memphis had killed that possibility.

However, after the other disappointments, Spurrier declared that the Volunteers could be proud of the fact that they were the 1996 Knox County champions. When UT fans took umbrage at Spurrier's comedy routine, he remarked that it was all in good fun, and poking fun at the opposition was common fare at booster club meetings. He said, "I would tell my funny little jokes to Gator boosters, and (FSU coach) Bobby Bowden would tell his corny little Gator jokes to the Seminole Clubs. Fans laugh and it's no big deal. But you tell one about Tennessee, and they think it's insulting or something. You'll never hear me complain about somebody telling a corny little joke about our team."

Before the 1997 UT game in "the Swamp," Spurrier's jibes at the Volunteers were a little more subtle than usual. He said, "It's a strong rivalry. I guess what makes it good is that I don't think Tennessee believes we're better than them." Most coaches feared that such a statement would have given a psychological edge to the opposition, but such comments from Spurrier seemed to incite anger that had a negative impact on the opposition by making them try too hard to make the ball coach eat his words.

After an unsuccessful two-year stint in the NFL, Spurrier returned to Neyland stadium to face Fulmer's Vols as the head ball coach of the South Carolina Gamecocks in 2005. The new Gamecocks coach professed that the NFL experience (two mediocre seasons as Washington Redskins head coach) had made him a wiser and more humble man, but he could still not resist taking some potshots at his long-time opponents in the Volunteer state.

In the week leading up to the late-October 2005 Tennessee-South Carolina game, Spurrier reminded the media that, going into the season, Tennessee had been ranked third in the nation in the Associated Press poll, and had been the over-whelming favorite to win the SEC title. However, as game day approached, his unheralded Gamecocks, who had received scant pre-season attention, actual-ly had a better record than the highly touted Vols. In comparing the two teams' dissimilar 2005 fates he asked, "Who would have thunk that"?

13
Revenge Against the Bulldogs

FLORIDA QUARTERBACK STEVE SPURRIER effectively sewed up the 1966 Heisman Trophy when he kicked a forty-yard field goal to beat Auburn at the end of that year's match between the Gators and the Tigers. After the victory over the Plainsmen, the undefeated Gators moved up to No. 7 in the national rankings and were a strong favorite to beat Georgia in their annual showdown in Jacksonville.

The Gators had been riding the late-game heroics of their star quarterback all season, and were seemingly poised to win their first ever Southeastern Conference championship. The most optimistic of the Gator faithful even envisioned a possible national championship.

The game plan worked like a charm. Spurrier was sacked six times, and Georgia's tremendous pass rush also caused him to throw three interceptions.

However, the Georgia Bulldogs were no slouches. They entered the game that *Florida Times-Union* columnist Bill Kastelz had labeled "the world's largest outdoor cocktail party" with a respectable 6-1 record, and Georgia had no intention of rolling over and playing dead for their heated rivals to the south.

The strength of that year's Georgia team was a strong defensive line that featured Bill Stanfill and George Patton. Bulldogs Coach Vince Dooley's strategy was to use his ferocious defensive front to put pressure on Spurrier to keep him from picking Georgia's defense to pieces. The game plan worked like a charm. Spurrier was sacked six times, and Georgia's tremendous pass rush also caused him to throw three interceptions as the Bulldogs recovered from a 10-6 halftime deficit to humiliate the Gators by a 27-10 score. The Gators' dreams of an undefeated season and SEC championship were destroyed on the field of the Gator Bowl that afternoon.

The 1966 defeat by Georgia was an embarrassment to the entire Florida team, but it was especially painful for Spurrier, their ultra-competitive quarterback. In the years that followed, the Bulldogs would come to understand how much that loss meant to Spurrier, and they would realize that he did not quickly forget what he considered to be a public humiliation.

The annual showdown between Georgia and Florida in Jacksonville's Gator Bowl had always been a marquee game on each team's schedule, but when Spurrier returned as head coach of the Gators in 1990, he told reporters in his pre-season assessment of the season that the Georgia-Florida contest was just another game on the Gators' schedule. The coach knew that comment would get under the skin of the Georgia faithful, who considered the game with the Gators as one of the biggest of the year.

In a further slap at the Bulldogs, Spurrier had labeled an early season game with perennial SEC and national powerhouse Alabama as the biggest game in 1990, his first year back in Gainesville as head coach of the Gators. Thus began a trend of Spurrier's getting the psychological edge over his rivals from Athens that would continue for the twelve years that he served as the Head Gator.

As Spurrier neared his first showdown with Georgia in 1990, his Gators were coming off three vastly different performances—a 45-3 thrashing at the hands of Tennessee in mid-October, followed by a 59-0 victory over lightweight Akron, and an astounding 48-7 flogging of the fourth-ranked Auburn Tigers.

Before the Gators took the field against the Bulldogs, he told his players that they "should beat Georgia by a bunch," and his words turned out to be prophetic as Florida rolled to a 38-7 victory. The lop-sided Florida victories over Georgia continued the next year as the Gators thumped the Bulldogs, 45-13. In the twelve years that Spurrier coached Florida they amazingly beat Georgia eleven times. No other coach has ever so completely dominated this heated border rivalry.

Not only did Spurrier win an amazing 92 per-cent of his encounters with Georgia, but the average score during his twelve games with the Bulldogs was 36-12 in favor of the Gators. Many of the Florida victories were by ridiculously wide margins: 38-7 in 1990, 45-13 in 1991, 52-14 in 1994, 52-17 in 1995, and 47-7 in 1996. When Spurrier returned to Florida, the Gators trailed in the Georgia series by eighteen games; but when a reporter asked him if he expected to even the series with Georgia, he replied seriously that he did not know if he would coach the Gators for eighteen years. The implication of that remark was that Spurrier had no intentions of losing any games to Georgia.

If the complete and utter domination of Georgia during the Spurrier era wasn't bad enough, the proud Georgia fans were further humiliated by the rhetoric they had to endure from the man they dubbed "the Evil Genius." Former Georgia football coach Vince Dooley, who served as athletic director while Spurrier coached the Gators, was the model of genial football coaches who were the norm in southern football before the brash and arrogant Spurrier arrived in Gainesville. Dooley observed that Spurrier's "got a way of irritating Georgia fans."

Dooley continued that the dislike of the Gators coach started with the Bulldogs' annual drubbings by Florida. Besides the winning it was the way in which he won. Dooley observed that, "On other occasions he (Spurrier) might make comments. He might score more points here in Athens. Instead of trying to slow the scoring down, it seems like he never tried to slow the scoring down. That really rubs people the wrong way. So it's a combination—the winning and the other things."

Upon hearing of Spurrier's retirement from the University of Florida in 2002, long-time Georgia broadcaster Larry Munson said, "He was good for the conference, even though he would say some things that would antagonize people, and he liked to stick the knife in and twist it on the Bulldogs."

The game that stuck in the craw of the Bulldog Nation more than any other during Spurrier's tenure in Gainesville was the 1995 game. The "world's largest outdoor cocktail" had traditionally been held at a neutral site, the Gator Bowl in Jacksonville, Florida. Over time the game had evolved into a huge social event in which Georgia and Florida boosters would spend the week preceding the game socializing in the host city. However, when Jacksonville was awarded an expansion team in the NFL, the city decided to upgrade the Gator Bowl (it would be renamed Alltel Stadium) to accommodate professional football.

During the two-year stadium renovation project, the annual Georgia/Florida games were moved to the respective teams' home stadiums. The first game was played at Florida's home field, Ben Hill Griffin Stadium, in 1994. The game was a complete rout for the Gators, who thumped their northern visitors, 52-14.

Georgia fans saw the 1995 encounter on their home field, Sanford Stadium, as an opportunity to get revenge for the 1994 debacle in The Swamp.

However, the Evil Genius' plans did not make room for any revenge on the part of the Bulldogs; and the Gators humiliated the proud Georgians 52-17 "between the hedges" in Athens.

As the Florida team traveled to the stadium on the morning of the game, Gator assistant coach Lawson Holland had remarked to Spurrier that no Georgia opponent had ever scored fifty points against the Bulldogs in Sanford Stadium. The assistant said, "Coach, if you get the chance, you ought to do it."

Spurrier did not exactly have to be cajoled into running up the score on Georgia, and as the game progressed it became apparent that the fifty-point barrier might possibly be breached.

Spurrier did not exactly have to be cajoled into running up the score on Georgia, and as the game progressed it became apparent that the fifty-point barrier might possibly be breached. With a little over a minute left in the game, Florida had the ball on Georgia's eight-yard line with a commanding 45-17 lead. The unwritten rules of football etiquette called for Florida to run out the clock so as not to further embarrass its vanquished opponent. However, the brash and arrogant Spurrier did not abide by the "old school" rules, and he called a pass play that resulted in an eight-yard touchdown pass, allowing the Gators to finish off a 52-17 victory.

After the game Spurrier told reporters that he had been told that no opponent had ever scored fifty points on Georgia's home field, and he wanted the Gators to be the first team to achieve that honor. To further enrage the Bulldog faithful, he remarked that, "They didn't seem to be too mad about the last touchdown." He said at the time that the last touchdown was scored, "They only had about five thousand left in the stadium."

14
A Sideshow
on the Sideline

THROUGHOUT HIS PLAYING CAREER and his early days in coaching, Spurrier had been a very competitive and emotional individual. As a college quarterback he had been entrusted with calling all of the offensive plays, and he still had that responsibility as an assistant coach in college and during his head-coaching days with the Tampa Bay Bandits, the Duke Blue Devils, the Florida Gators, and the South Carolina Gamecocks.

When he called successful plays as a coach, he would celebrate on the sideline with upraised arms. Unsuccessful plays would bring a scowl and a look of anguish. Disastrous plays could bring a toss of his ever-present visor. Before he became head coach at Florida, however, his sideline antics attracted little attention since his previous teams attracted little publicity.

As soon as Spurrier burst on the scene at Florida, his Gators became extremely successful, and their games were frequently featured on national television. They were an exciting team to watch, and Spurrier's sideline gyrations and facial expressions were an added treat. Cameras loved him, and it's probably a good guess the feeling was mutual.

The sideline theatrics, which had previously only entertained fans in the stadium who were sitting close to the bench where Spurrier was performing, were now broadcast throughout the nation to fans who had never seen such a whirling dervish on the sideline. The television networks quickly discovered the entertainment value of the coach's sideline gesturing, and always had one camera dedicated to following the coach's every movement throughout the course of the game. *Sports Illustrated* always had a photographer assigned to cover all of Spurrier's actions during games that they covered.

Most college coaches behave like a corporate CEO on the sideline during games, bottling whatever emotions they experience inside. They delegate the nitty-gritty of sideline coaching to their offensive and defensive coaches, and try to insure that the right players are in the game at any given time.

Since Spurrier did not fit this mold of the typical coach, he became the center of attention during Florida games. Some observers said that Spurrier was so active on the sideline because he was not only the head coach, but also because he functioned as his team's quarterback coach and offensive coordinator. His antics on the field have been compared to those of a basketball coach, rather than a football coach.

After Florida walloped traditional college football power Alabama, 35-0, during the 1991 season, Spurrier received a letter from a fan concerned about his sideline demeanor. The Gators fan told the coach that he needed to calm down on the sideline because he appeared to be too stressed and emotional during the games. The booster pointed out that other coaches did not act like Spurrier, and he was worried that his coach's frenetic sideline manner would cause him to burn out too quickly.

As the Gators coach reflected upon the fan's concern, he thought that maybe the fan had a legitimate point. The Gators had a game the following week at Syracuse, and Spurrier made a conscious decision that week to let the assistant coaches do all the yelling at the players during their preparations for the Orangemen. The head Gator acted like he perceived other head coaches acted during the road trip to New York and during the game itself. When the game was played, Spurrier characterized the players' performance as being like a bunch of zombies, and Syracuse soundly defeated Florida, 38-21.

The return to the natural style worked like a charm, and Spurrier's Gators won the remainder of their games that year to finish with a 10-1 record.

After the game Spurrier apologized to the players, and told them that the calm and collected style might work for other coaches but it sure "doesn't work for me." He told the players that he thought he could only be effective by using his natural style, which included being emotional on every play and constantly yelling at them. The return to the natural style worked like a charm, and Spurrier's Gators won the remainder of their games that year to finish with a 10-1 record and claim their first Southeastern Conference championship.

Throughout the remainder of his coaching career, the Head Ball Coach utilized his "natural" style of coaching. This style featured yanking off his headset after plays that didn't go his way, pulling off his visor (and giving the visor a fling if the play was

56

especially bad), rubbing his fingers through his hair or across his brow, exaggerated grimaces which seemed to indicate extreme pain, and constantly yelling instructions to any player whose performance caused the coach displeasure.

15
Poor, Poor Peyton

PEYTON MANNING FINISHED HIS four-year career at the University of Tennessee with status secured as one of the greatest quarterbacks in college history, mainly because of his great passing exploits. But there were two things conspicuously missing from Manning's treasure chest of exploits when he left Rocky Top: a Heisman Trophy and, even worse than that, a victory over Florida. That's right; a Manning-quarterbacked team never beat a Spurrier-coached team during the former's four years in Knoxville.

After the Southeastern Conference split into two divisions in 1992, the Gators and Volunteers emerged as the two strongest programs in the Eastern

Conference, and the winner of their annual show-down in September was the favorite to represent the Eastern Division in the SEC championship game.

In Manning's freshman year of 1994, Todd Helton, who would later become an outstanding baseball player for the Colorado Rockies, was the starting Tennessee quarterback; and Manning did not enter the game until after the Gators had built a 24-0 halftime lead. Manning shared playing time in the second half with fellow frosh phenom Brandon Stewart, but neither of the rookie signal callers could put any points on the scoreboard as the Volunteers suffered an embarrassing 31-0 loss to Florida at Neyland Stadium.

The shutout loss was Tennessee's first since Georgia and Herschel Walker had beaten them, 44-0, in 1981. Although young Manning complet-ed only three of five passes for twenty-seven yards, he provided some momentary excitement for Vols' fans with three and one-half minutes to play, when he threw an apparent touchdown pass to receiver Nilo Silvan. The home team scoreboard exploded in a crescendo of fireworks as Silvan ran into the Gators' end zone. However, in a precursor to later frustrations that Manning would suffer against the

Gators, the officials ruled that the quarterback had crossed the line of scrimmage before throwing the pass, and the score was nullified.

When the series resumed in Gainesville in Manning's sophomore year in 1995, the sophomore signal caller's luck against the Gators seemed to turn. He opened the game with a seventy-two-yard pass to wide receiver Joey Kent, and shortly thereafter hit Marcus Nash with a touchdown pass to give the Vols a 7-0 lead. While the 1994 Florida game had been a nightmare for the Volunteers, the first half of the 1995 game was a beautiful dream. Manning conducted a quarterback clinic as he sliced and diced the Florida defense, pushing Tennessee to a 30-7 lead just before halftime. Spurrier, on the other side of the field, was just getting warmed up, however.

The Gators scored a touchdown just before halftime to cut the UT lead to 30-14; and the second-half script reverted back to the nightmare scenario. Florida completely throttled the Volunteers' offense in the second half, and their own offense scored touchdowns on six consecutive second-half possessions as they annihilated Tennessee, 62-37. Counting the touchdown at the end of the first half, the Gators rolled up seven touchdowns in slightly over thirty minutes of clock time.

The sixty-two points was the most that the Vols had given up since being clobbered by Duke, 70-0, back in 1893. The Gators rang up 584 yards of offense on the proud UT defense, and Gator quarterback Danny Wuerffel completed twenty-nine of thirty-nine passes for 381 yards. Manning finished with twenty-three completions in thirty-six attempts including two touchdown passes, but he was completely ineffective in the second half. Shell-shocked Tennessee Coach Phillip Fulmer said after the game that the Vols had been able to execute their game plan in the first half, but in the second half the Vols secondary "looked like 'Ned and the Third Reader' " as the Gators' offensive schemes turned them completely around.

When the 1996 showdown with Florida rolled around, the Volunteers were loaded with talent, even more than the season before, and Manning had emerged as a pre-season favorite to win the Heisman Trophy. Most of the college football record crowd of 107,608 that jammed Neyland Stadium expected to see their beloved Volunteers get revenge for their past humiliations at the hands of Spurrier's Gators. Plus, Manning's Heisman chances could be greatly enhanced by a strong performance in front of a huge nationwide TV audience.

This time, however, it was Florida that got the fast start, basically picking up where it had left off in 1995, scoring touchdowns, one right after another. In fact, the Gators scored their first two touchdowns in the game's first five minutes, and just four minutes deep into the second quarter had extended the lead to 35-0. Manning ended the first half with four interceptions, and that effectively ended any mention of Manning and Heisman in the same sentence.

Besides the four interceptions, a harassed Manning had contributed numerous poor play-calling decisions and erratic throws to the first-half debacle. Although Tennessee mounted a strong second-half comeback, they still finished on the short end of a 35-29 score. Ironically, Florida quarterback Danny Wuerffel, who engineered the Gators' early scoring drives, would go on to win the Heisman Trophy in 1996.

At the end of the game a frustrated Manning explained, "Nobody wanted to win this game more than I did. I knew there was going to be a game like this for me sometime in my career. I'm just sorry it was against Florida. I feel so badly for so

At the end of the game a frustrated Manning explained, "Nobody wanted to win this game more than I did. I knew there was going to be a game like this for me sometime in my career."

many people this game meant so much to. I'm sorry I played the way I did."

Peyton's dad, legendary Ole Miss quarterback Archie Manning, related after the game that he had once thrown six interceptions against Tennessee in Neyland Stadium in 1968. Archie explained that "It's going to happen to you. It's inevitable with everyone. When you play a defense like Florida, it can happen."

After Peyton Manning's junior season, there was a great deal of speculation that the Vols' signal caller would forego his final season of college eligibility, and play the 1997 season as a professional in the National Football League. After a long and drawn out decision-making process, the UT quarterback finally announced in December 1996 that he would return for his final season with the Volunteers, a decision reached much to the delight of the Tennessee faithful.

When Spurrier was asked to give his two cents as to why he believed Manning had decided to return for one more year at UT, the head Gator said Manning's decision was obviously the result of his desire to be named the most valuable player in the Citrus Bowl for three consecutive seasons. The Citrus Bowl was the post-season destination of the team that finished second in the SEC's Eastern Division, and Tennessee's inability to beat Florida had insured its participation in the Citrus Bowl in Manning's sophomore and junior years, rather than the more prestigious Sugar Bowl trip for the SEC champion which the Gators had enjoyed. Manning's explanation for returning for his senior year was to enjoy the college experience for one more year, and also to lead the Vols to a possible SEC and national championship.

As the Vols' annual showdown with the Florida Gators approached in 1997, it was apparent that the Gators would again be an obstacle to UT achieving their team goals, and that a strong performance by Manning would also give his last-ditch Heisman Trophy aspirations a major boost. Both teams came into the 1997 game with undefeated records, and, as in the previous three years, the winner of the September showdown would have the inside track to represent the Eastern Division of the SEC in the league championship game.

The Gators took an early 7-0 lead, and shortly thereafter Manning figured prominently in the play that proved to be the turning point in the game. After the Gators had scored the first touchdown, Manning led UT on a drive that reached the Florida

24-yard line with less than half a minute to go in the first quarter. At that point the Vols faced a third and eleven. As the play developed, the Florida defense blitzed, with cornerback Elijah Williams and defensive end Ed Chester bearing down on Manning. The harassed Vol quarterback threw a pass that was intercepted by Gator strong safety Tony George, who stepped in front of the intended Tennessee receiver, and did not stop running until he had gone 89 yards for a Gator touchdown.

Although Manning would wind up with 353 passing yards on 29-of-52 passing, the Vols never seriously threatened the Gators after that ill-timed interception.

Although Manning would wind up with 353 passing yards on 29-of-52 passing, the Vols never seriously threatened the Gators after that ill-timed interception, and suffered their fifth straight loss to their rivals from Gainesville. Final score: Florida 33, Tennessee 20.

After the game UT Coach Fulmer said, "I think Peyton did all right," but the senior signal caller was painfully disappointed by his fourth straight loss to the Spurrier-led Gators. The disconsolate quarterback said, "It bothers me that we never beat Florida. I needed to play well for us to win the game, and I didn't. I apologize for that. You hate to lose. I probably hate to lose more than I like to win. But Florida's a great team, and you have to give them a lot of credit. I'm sure Coach Spurrier will go on and make a few more jokes, and that's fine, he can go on and do that."

16
Me and Phil

DURING SPURRIER'S TENURE AS coach of the Florida Gators, his primary obstacle to achieving supremacy in the Eastern Division of the SEC was Tennessee. Between the time that Phillip Fulmer became head coach of the Volunteers in 1993 and his last game against the Spurrier-coached Gators in 2001, UT lost only twenty games. Seven of those were to the Gators.

When Spurrier made his innumerable jokes about the Vols, Fulmer generally did not respond. However, on a few occasions the head Volunteer shot some zingers back at his coaching rival. After Florida was humiliated by Nebraska in the 1995 national championship game, the Gators tumbled from second to third in the final coaches' poll, and the Volunteers moved up to the No. 2 position. The Gators' demise was caused by the fact that one coach had voted Florida thirteenth. Spurrier always suspected Fulmer was the culprit, but when reporters asked Phillip, he said that he had voted the Gators third. When Spurrier was asked where he put Tennessee in the 1996 pre-season poll, he said, "high—very high."

When Spurrier first left Florida to coach the Washington Redskins after the 2001 season, Fulmer was asked if he would miss his old Gator rival. The head Vol replied, "I'm glad he's in Washington. I won't miss him." As the first Florida-Tennessee game after Spurrier's departure approached in September 2002, Fulmer was asked how the Head Ball Coach's absence would change the nature of the Florida-Tennessee rivalry. Fulmer's only comment was that "it's probably not as annoying."

During Spurrier's first spring at the helm of the South Carolina Gamecocks, in 2005, off-the-field problems with players ignited a major skirmish between the old rivals. When Spurrier was asked about criminal charges being dropped against Gamecocks' receiver Syvelle Newton, the coach replied, "I guess at one time somebody accused

Newton of slapping him or something, but this was not a full-blown fight. If you want to read about some full-blown fights, read about the Tennessee players, not our guys."

Tennessee had had eleven players arrested in the previous year, including four who had been arrested that April on charges stemming from two separate on-campus fights. Fulmer answered his long-time rival by saying, "He needs to take care of his own house and leave mine to me. He's got plenty of issues over there, I'm sure, to deal with. I don't give a (expletive) one way or the other what anybody says, except people that count."

Spurrier, who obviously enjoyed getting Fulmer agitated, laughed upon hearing his remarks and said, "Sometimes a little publicity is good, I believe. I'm glad Fulmer said something. I'm glad he's listening to us. In the past I don't think he'd worry much about what a South Carolina coach said, do you?"

When Spurrier returned to the SEC after his failed experiment in pro football, the SEC media were anxious to stir up a controversy between the old rivals at the media days event in the summer of 2005. Fulmer jokingly feigned disappointment at having his old rival back in the conference by saying, "When I first heard he was coming back, I said, 'Ah, crap.' " The Vols' coach then went on to say, "I think he brings a lot of personality to the conference, obviously, and he's a great football coach and great competitor."

When Fulmer was asked if he had any advice for Spurrier upon his re-entry into the league, his tongue-in-cheek reply was "I don't have any advice for Steve. He seems to have all the answers."

17
Where Have All the
Blue Chippers Gone?

E VER SINCE THE GEORGIA BULLDOGS ruined quarterback Steve Spurrier's dream of leading his Florida Gators to an undefeated season and the Southeastern Conference championship in 1966, Spurrier has not been a big fan of Florida's cross-border rival. During his twelve years of coaching the Gators, he beat the Bulldogs eleven times, and some of the defeats were by margins that embarrassed the proud Georgia program.

One year before Spurrier returned to Gainesville as head coach of his alma mater in 1990, the Bulldogs hired former quarterback Ray Goff, who quarterbacked them to the 1976 SEC championship, to replace the retiring Vince Dooley as head football coach. While Spurrier's return to Florida was an overwhelming success, with the Gators dominating the SEC during most of his tenure in Gainesville and winning one national championship, Goff's Georgia teams won less than 60 percent of their games during his seven seasons. Spurrier's Florida teams beat Goff's Bulldogs in all six of their encounters with Florida, averaging forty-one points to only seventeen for Georgia. The Gators won the last two Spurrier/Goff showdowns in 1994 and 1995 by scores of 52-14 and 52-17, respectively.

While Georgia fans viewed Spurrier as an arrogant brat (and evil offensive genius), Florida fans made fun of good-ole-boy Goff, frequently referring to him as "Ray Goof."

While Georgia fans viewed Spurrier as an arrogant brat (and evil offensive genius), Florida fans made fun of good-ole-boy Goff, frequently referring to him as "Ray Goof." Spurrier was a master at playing mind games that befuddled Goff and the Bulldogs year-after-year. Florida had beaten Goff's Bulldogs six consecutive times as the 1995 game approached, and when Spurrier was asked if he was concerned about playing Georgia, "The Evil Genius" answered with a question of his own, "Is Ray Goff still coaching there?"

In the summer of 1991 Spurrier read in a Georgia fan magazine that the Bulldogs had recruited better than anyone in the SEC during Goff's tenure in Athens. The recruiting guru had ranked the Gators' recruiting efforts as fifth-best in the ten-team conference. The article's implication that Goff had out-recruited Spurrier irked the ultra-competitive Gator, and after the Gators waxed Georgia by a 45-13 score in their game in October 1991, the head Gator asked a Florida booster club in Jacksonville, "How is it when Georgia signs people, they get the 'best' players, but when we play, we've got the 'best' players? Georgia has signed a lot of good players, but something just happens to them at Georgia, I guess."

18
Free Shoes University

FLORIDA AND FLORIDA STATE are heated rivals, and during many of the years when Steve Spurrier coached the Gators, their annual November showdown had major national implications as well as being the source of bragging rights in the football-crazy Sunshine State (not counting Miami, of course).

With its favorable weather and large population, the state of Florida was a recruiting hotbed and regularly stocked national title contenders in Gainesville, Tallahassee, and Miami. Florida State had won its first national championship in 1993, and the Seminoles were still basking in the glory of their achievement in the summer of 1994, when player agents financed a $6,000 shopping spree for four players at a Tallahassee area Foot Locker store. After accounts of the shopping excursion (which violated NCAA rules) made national headlines, FSU suspended the four players involved.

Florida Coach Steve Spurrier, who already had a well-deserved reputation for tweaking the psyche of opponents, had a field day with the Seminoles' woes. Shortly after the incident, the head Gator asked the Polk County Gator Club if they knew what "FSU" stood for. Spurrier's reply was that FSU was an acronym for "Free Shoes University."

He poured more gas on the fire by observing that, "We've always heard rumors about them. They've beaten us four out of the last five years in recruiting. Heck, maybe they're the greatest recruiters in the world. But maybe there are other reasons that those guys go there. Those guys always say they feel 'more comfortable' going to FSU. Well, maybe we're starting to realize what 'more comfortable' means." Spurrier went on to observe that the cars in the FSU players' parking lot seemed to have an awful lot of shine on them. He concluded with: "I'm not saying anybody broke any rules. I'm just saying that there was a feeling of, well, those kids are driving awfully nice cars."

When University of Florida President John Lombardi heard about Spurrier's remarks he said, "The University of Florida has no standing to criticize any other university" (a reference to the fact that the Gators had themselves been put on NCAA probation in 1990). Lombardi continued by saying, "The good thing about Coach Spurrier's insights is that nothing is ever a mystery." Florida Athletic Director Jeremy Foley chimed in with, "We should not make those comments. We've been there before. We know what it's like to be on the other side."

Despite Lombardi's and Foley's comments, Spurrier never retracted his remarks. In a 1995 profile of Spurrier in *The Sporting News*, sportswriter Douglas S. Looney opined that Spurrier's stance was that "If the handcuffs fit, wear them." In his last dig at FSU in the scandal, the Gators' coach purported to see a silver lining for himself in the debacle. He remarked in the fall of 1994, "It used to be that I was the most hated man in Tallahassee. Now it's the NCAA investigator."

19
Darth Visor

LEGENDARY SOUTHERN FOOTBALL COACHES seem to become identified with their headwear. Alabama's Paul "Bear" Bryant, who dominated the Southeastern Conference and college football in the 1960's and 1970's, was identified by his trademark houndstooth hat. No single SEC coach dominated the 1980's, but Florida's Steve Spurrier, and his trademark visor, ruled the roost in the 1990's.

While the reserved Bryant would wear his houndstooth hat as he stood stoically on the 'Bama sideline where he presided over a seemingly endless stream of Crimson Tide victories; the volatile, visor-wearing Spurrier would wildly gesticulate on the sideline as his Gators ran up previously unheard-of point totals and victories during the 1990's and the first two years of the twenty-first century.

Spurrier himself attached little significance to the visor. He maintained that since at least half of his games were played in the Sunshine State, the visor was a useful device to keep the sun out of his eyes. As his Florida Gators became ultra-successful during his tenure in Gainesville, legions of non-Florida fans enjoyed watching Spurrier express his displeasure with an unsuccessful play with a violent heave of his headgear. In poking fun at his visor tossing, Spurrier once said, "I have learned to throw it up in the air a little bit because I got some serious grass stains on it about three years ago."

After Spurrier accepted the head-coaching job at South Carolina after the 2004 football season, a Columbia sporting goods store reported brisk sales of a Spurrier-type visor in the Gamecocks' garnet and black colors. When Mississippi State's feeble offense gained only 205 yards against Auburn in a 2005 game, Spurrier's boyhood friend and *Tennessean* sports columnist Joe Biddle decried the inept offensive performance by declaring, "Spurrier can throw his visor that far."

Douglas Looney wrote in *The Sporting News* that Spurrier used the visor to set himself apart from other coaches. Before the 1994 Florida-Florida State game in Tallahassee, Spurrier was told that FSU boosters were including a visor-throwing ceremony as part of the pre-game activities at Doak Campbell Stadium. The amused head Gator chuckled that he "didn't know I was that important to the Seminoles."

20
Ruffians in Tallahassee

THE INTENSE RIVALRY BETWEEN Florida and Florida State did not require any extra spice, but Spurrier was able to enliven it throughout his tenure with the Gators.

The 1996 Gators team was one of his most talented, and they were ranked No. 1 in the nation as they entered their annual showdown with FSU in November. Gators quarterback Danny Wuerffel (who went on to win the 1996 Heisman Trophy) had had an outstanding season, and the Seminoles believed that keeping intense pressure on Wuerffel was the key to beating Florida. Before the game, FSU's All American defensive end Peter Boulware said, "The only way to stop Wuerffel is to make sure he's on his back with the ball."

The Seminoles did a superb job of carrying out their defensive strategy; and the Gators, who came into the game averaging forty-nine points per game, were held to only twenty-one points as they lost by three points. During the course of the game, the Seminoles were penalized three times for roughing the quarterback. After the game Spurrier said that the three penalties that were assessed against FSU were not nearly enough, and that they had been guilty of numerous other late hits that were not called. He also accused Florida State of "playing dirty" throughout the contest.

After the Gators won the host spot in the 1997 Sugar Bowl by defeating Alabama for the 1996 SEC championship, the Sugar Bowl announced that Florida's bowl rival would be their cross-state foe, the Seminoles. As soon as the pairing was announced, Spurrier began his media campaign of accusing FSU of dirty play. His harping about the Seminoles' "dirty play" put the officiating crew on notice to protect his star quarterback from a recurrence of what had happened in Tallahassee.

Spurrier's tactics also proved to be a brilliant ruse that distracted FSU coach Bobby Bowden from pre-game planning as he spent a good deal of time responding to Spurrier's accusations of dirty play.

With the officials on notice and the Seminoles pre-occupied with Spurrier's accusations, the Gators cruised to their only national championship with a 52-20 romp over the Seminoles.

In 2001 Spurrier also accused the Seminoles of playing dirty in a 37-13 Florida victory. During the course of the game, Florida running back Earnest Graham had come hobbling off the field; and when Spurrier asked him about his injury, Graham said that Florida State linebacker Darnell Dockett had twisted his leg after he had been tackled. After the game Spurrier repeated the player's accusations to the media, and said that the Florida coaching staff would review the game films to ascertain what had happened. Spurrier added, "I'm not accusing anybody of anything, but if that did occur, something needs to be done. We can't watch guys twist guys' legs after they are on the ground and so forth. But we'll let the proper people take review of how he got hurt."

After reviewing the game film, Spurrier said, "It didn't clearly show the guy, but the guy was sort of doing something down there. I hate to bring it up, but still, I've got to say something on behalf of Earnest Graham." Further ammunition was added to the debate when a report in the *St. Petersburg Times* said that Dockett was overheard after the game asking his teammates, "Did you see what I did to Earnest Graham?"

Rather than defusing the situation, Spurrier added fuel to the fire in the week following the game by asking, "Would I say it surprises me an FSU player did that? No, it doesn't surprise me. It doesn't surprise me Bowden won't do anything. That's the way they do business at FSU. It's the way they run their show there. It doesn't surprise me at all." Florida State's athletic director, Dave Hart, summed up the Seminoles' response to the Graham-Dockett affair when he said, "I think Spurrier is a very good football coach, and he has an outstanding football team this year. But it probably would be good if somebody would just spank him and put him to bed and hope he wakes up all grown up."

21
It's Hard to Be Humble

EVEN AS A YOUNG ATHLETE, Steve Spurrier had a confident air that some people called cockiness or arrogance. As an All-State high school basketball player, his flashy style of play, which included behind-the-back passes and between-the-legs dribbling, reinforced his reputation as arrogant, and opposing fans loved to harass the confident youngster.

The taunts of the opposing fans only made the young Spurrier more determined to succeed, and that was a trait that he has maintained ever since. As a high school athlete, Spurrier earned All-State honors in football, basketball, and baseball; so his confidence was based upon the overwhelming success that he achieved in his athletic career. His successful football career at the University of Florida, where he was an All-American quarterback and Heisman Trophy winner, only increased his confidence.

Former University of Florida sports information director Norm Carlson said that Spurrier's confidence came from the fact that he had "no sense of failure." Carlson said that Spurrier absolutely thought he would be successful in any endeavor. While most "old school" football coaches would "poor mouth" their team's chances for success and exaggerate the strength of their opponent, Spurrier would try to give an honest assessment of his team's capabilities. The Head Ball Coach explained, "Maybe I act and talk differently than most coaches do. If we have a team that has got a chance to win the conference, I'll say we have got a chance to win the conference championship." He went on to say, "I may talk a little more confidently than some coaches—but I certainly don't ever mean to insult or brag."

When Spurrier left Duke in 1990 to return to his alma mater in Gainesville, he realized that departing Gators Coach Galen Hall had left a great deal of talent, and he told the press that he was optimistic about his team's chances. Spurrier said that this struck some observers of SEC football as being arrogant, and he was labeled as an arrogant loud-mouth. One sportswriter observed that if anyone doubted how good a coach Spurrier was, all they had to do was ask him.

A *Sporting News* profile of Spurrier in 1995 said that Spurrier's arrogance was confirmed by his reaction to criticism. When he was asked if he agreed with much of the criticism of himself, Spurrier replied, "Not much, to tell you the truth." While at Florida, Spurrier kept a quote from former UCLA basketball coach John Wooden in his office that says, "The more successful you are, the more you are criticized."

Long-time rival Phillip Fulmer of the Tennessee Volunteers described Spurrier as "a very competitive person who can be egotistical, arrogant, and whiny." Fulmer continued, "I accept that about him and go on about my business."

When Auburn coach Tommy Tuberville was asked about Spurrier's arrogance when he resigned from Florida to take the Redskins job, Tuberville said, "He was a little different, he was outspoken. But you can be pretty outspoken when you're beating everybody's butt like he was."

When Steve Spurrier, Jr. was asked about his father's reputation for arrogance, he said that he saw his dad as confident—not arrogant. The younger Spurrier said, "I'd rather be arrogant about winning than depressed about losing." Georgia Coach Mark Richt, whose only loss in 2001 was to Florida and Spurrier, said that Spurrier's "personality brought a lot of excitement. He just got people riled up and ready to go. He got the fans riled up. He got the players riled up, his own and the other teams."

After two unsuccessful seasons as coach of the Washington Redskins, Spurrier was more humble than usual when he returned to college coaching

After two unsuccessful seasons as coach of the Washington Redskins, Spurrier was more humble than usual when he returned to college coaching with the South Carolina Gamecocks in 2005. Knowing that he initially faced diminished expectations with the Gamecocks, the coach said, "I don't think you should ever say anything's impossible, but we don't need to be talking too big right now."

During the press conference announcing his introduction as the new South Carolina coach, Spurrier said that he had learned a lot of humility during his stint in the NFL. In referring to his time at Florida, he said, "Maybe I ran my mouth more than I should, but I've seen some other coaches that are winning pretty big right now and winning by big scores, and sometimes they talk too much, too. Human nature causes you to maybe feel like you have more answers than you do when you've got a really good team."

When he was asked about the "swagger" that characterized his Florida teams, the slightly more humble coach allowed that with South Carolina, it would be more of a controlled swagger. He continued, "If we've got real good players that can score a lot of points, then we can have a swagger. But you've got to do that first."

22
Love Me, Love My Dog

RECRUITING HAS BEEN CALLED the lifeblood of college sports in that it allows schools to maintain a steady flow of athletic talent into their institutions. Although some coaches aren't especially enamored of having to grovel before a seventeen- or eighteen-year-old high school hot-shot, they all realize that recruiting is a necessary evil.

One of the best offensive line recruits in Florida's 1999 recruiting season was Justin Smiley of tiny Brooklet, Georgia. When the recruiting wars began, Smiley was leaning toward going to South Carolina because the recruit's cousin had once played for South Carolina Coach Lou Holtz during Holtz's tenure at Notre Dame. After attending the

After an intensive recruitment of the young Georgian, Florida decided to send in the head Gator, Steve Spurrier, to seal the deal.

USC football camp for two summers, the youngster was even more inclined to sign with South Carolina.

However, an all-out recruiting effort by the Florida Gators soon convinced young Smiley that he would have a brighter future as a Gator than as a Gamecock. After an intensive recruitment of the young Georgian, Florida decided to send in the head Gator, Steve Spurrier, to seal the deal. Spurrier, who is known for his sideline attire of a golf shirt and the trademark visor atop his head, showed up at the Smiley household in a fine, shiny new suit.

When he came through the front door of the prized recruit's house in his sartorial splendor, the coach was met by the family pooch, a 120-pound charcoal Labrador named "Drake." Spurrier did not think dog hair would do anything to enhance his new suit, and he nudged "Drake" away from him. His unfriendliness to "Drake" did not go unnoticed by Smiley's mother (who happened to be a lifelong Alabama fan), and after the Florida coach concluded his visit, the mother remarked to her son, "He doesn't like your dog. The other coaches played with the dog, but Spurrier didn't want him touching him."

The conventional wisdom of coaches is that the mother is generally the most important person in the recruiting decision, and this proved to be correct as Smiley eventually signed with Alabama and had an outstanding career with the Crimson Tide before continuing his career with the San Diego Chargers.

23
You Can't Score
Too Many Points

A FOOTBALL COACHES' MAXIM IS that it is not gentlemanly, or smart, to continue piling on the points after an opponent has been hopelessly defeated. Not only is it unseemly to continue to run up the score on an outmanned foe, but an embarrassed opponent could be motivated for revenge the next time you face him.

The Duchess of Windsor once proclaimed that you could never be too rich or too thin, and the iconoclastic Steve Spurrier believed that you could never have too many points in a football game. Other coaches' conservative ball-control offenses generally led to low-scoring games, but Spurrier's wide open "fun and gun" offense was designed to score a lot of points, and he reveled in offensive fireworks.

Spurrier's Florida teams could never be accused of discriminatory practices in their scoring; they rang up high point totals on just about everyone. His first game as head coach of the Gators (a 50-7 mauling of Oklahoma State) was indicative of what awaited the opposition during the twelve years that he coached in Gainesville. Some of Spurrier's most one-sided victories were: 59-0 vs. Akron in 1990; 59-21 vs. San Jose State in 1991; 58-3 vs. LSU in 1993; 70-21 vs. New Mexico State in 1994; 63-7 vs. South Carolina in 1995; 65-0 vs. Kentucky in 1996; and 82-6 vs. Central Michigan in 1997. Spurrier's former coach, boss, and opponent Pepper Rodgers said that "embarrassment is part of the game to him."

After being humiliated by Spurrier in "the Swamp" in 1994 by a 52-14 score, Georgia Bulldog fans were looking for revenge when the Gators played the 1995 game in Athens. Before the game Gator assistant coach Lawson Holland remarked to Spurrier that no opposing team had ever scored fifty points on the Bulldogs' home field. With slightly over a minute to play the Gators, who had a 45-17 lead, had the ball on the Bulldogs' eight-yard line. Rather than calling a couple of running plays to consume the remaining time, Spurrier ordered up an eight-yard touchdown pass that increased the final score to 52-17.

Unlike the Tennessee fans, Volunteers Coach Phillip Fulmer was philosophical about Spurrier's actions. Fulmer said, "I don't blame Spurrier for throwing at the end. It's our job to stop it."

In 1997 the Bulldogs handed Spurrier his only defeat in twelve games against his arch-rival with a 37-17 thrashing in their annual showdown in Jacksonville's Gator Bowl. The next year the ball coach was out for revenge, and his Gators enjoyed a 31-7 lead over the Bulldogs with just thirty-eight seconds remaining in the game. Rather than sit on the twenty-four-point margin, however, Spurrier called an end around play to give the Gators another touchdown and increase the final margin to 38-7. "Old school" former Georgia coach Vince Dooley, who was Georgia's athletic director in 1998, said he was shocked by Spurrier's action.

In 1995 the Gators led Tennessee by a score of 55-30 late in the game in Gainesville. Spurrier infuriated the Volunteer fans by calling a twenty-yard touchdown pass to make it 62-30. Unlike the Tennessee fans, Volunteers Coach Phillip Fulmer was philosophical about Spurrier's actions. Fulmer said, "I don't blame Spurrier for throwing at the end.

94

It's our job to stop it. If we can get sixty-two on him one day, I'll get it."

Prior to the 1995 season, Spurrier met Houston Cougars Coach Kim Helton at a golf tournament sponsored by the football coaches' association. The Cougars, who were Florida's opening-game opponent that year, were coming off a disastrous season in which they had only won one game, and had finished among the worst college teams in three defensive categories. Spurrier told fellow Florida graduate Helton, "Kim, now I've seen y'all's film and I'll tell you, we're going to have a hard time keeping it under sixty."

Former Kentucky Coach Bill Curry was victimized several times by lopsided defeats at the hands of Spurrier's offensive juggernauts. After being hammered by scores of 73-7 in 1994, 42-7 in 1995, and 65-0 in 1995 (his final year), Curry was asked if the horrendous scoring assaults made Spurrier unpopular in the coaching ranks. The Wildcats' coach said, "I don't know if he's unpopular among coaches, but if he is it's probably because coaches don't like getting beat."

After Curry's departure from Kentucky, Hal Mumme was hired as the new coach of the Wildcats, partially because he had a reputation of running a wide-open, high-scoring offense similar to the ones that Spurrier had at Florida. According to several observers, Spurrier did not like the fact that someone who was not wearing a visor was putting up Spurrier-like offensive numbers, and being compared to the Florida offensive mastermind. Therefore, when Spurrier had a 52-31 lead on the Wildcats in 2000 with only thirteen seconds remaining in the game, the ball coach called a play that resulted in a forty-three-yard touchdown pass. After the game Spurrier proudly proclaimed, "I called that last pass. They were trying to run up their stats, so we worked on ours. They can get mad when we go to Kentucky next year."

When it came to scoring outlandish point totals, Spurrier even had no compassion for the halt and the lame. When Florida played the Vanderbilt Commodores in Gainesville in 2001, Vandy Coach Woody Widenhofer was trying desperately to hang onto his job at the graveyard of SEC coaches. If the embattled Widenhofer expected any mercy from Spurrier's Gators, he was not long in being disillusioned of such a fantasy. The Floridians scored twenty-four points in the first quarter and cruised to a 71-13 thrashing of the hapless Commodores. Although he had a seemingly safe 71-0 lead in the fourth quarter, Spurrier still had his quarterbacks throwing the ball all over the field.

Spurrier's only loss to the Mississippi State Bulldogs came in 2000, in Starkville. The Gators were completely outplayed as their offense had a school record minus seventy-eight rushing yards in the game, while the Gator defense yielded 517 yards to the Bulldogs. The loss snapped a seventy-two-game winning streak for the Gators against unranked teams, and the Bulldog fans stormed the field after the momentous upset victory. Although Mississippi State came into the 2001 game yielding only sixty-eight passing yards per game to lead the nation, any Bulldog ideas of pulling another upset were quickly dispelled as the Gators bolted to a 21-0 lead in the first quarter and coasted to a 52-0 victory.

The Gators were not impressed with Mississippi State's highly regarded pass defense, which they shredded for 507 yards through the air on their way to 640 total yards. The Gators were leading the Bulldogs 45-0 with only 1:45 to play, when Spurrier called for a last-minute, twenty-three-yard touchdown pass to increase the final margin to 52-0. When asked why he went for the last touchdown, the puckish Gator coach said it was for revenge for the Gators' student manager who had been jostled in the 2000 post-game victory party in Starkville.

When Spurrier was asked about his penchant for running up the score his answer was, "I hope I'm accused of running it up as long as I'm a coach because I believe that teams that can score a lot of points will score a lot, and teams that can't score a lot will whine and moan about those who can."

24
Modesty Has Its Place

THE CONVENTIONAL WISDOM AMONG football coaches is that you never brag about yourself or your team. Steve Spurrier turned that conventional wisdom on its ear. In analyzing his success as a football coach he observed, "If you want to be successful, you have to do it the way everybody else does it, and do it a lot better—or you have to do it differently. I can't outwork anybody, and I can't coach the off-tackle play better than anybody else. So I figured I'd try to coach some different ball plays, and instead of poor-mouthing my team, I'd try to build it up to the point where the players think, 'Coach believes we're pretty good, by golly, let's go prove it.' "

Quarterbacks loved to play in his wide-open offense, and he frequently was able to recruit a large number of outstanding high school quarterback prospects. However, only one quarterback can play at a time, and the quarterbacks who did not receive sufficient playing time under Spurrier's tutelage frequently transferred to other schools. When the Head Ball Coach was asked about the propensity of his quarterbacks to transfer to other schools, he matter-of-factly observed, "I can't make star players out of all of 'em."

While Spurrier was serving as Red Wilson's offensive coordinator at Duke in the early 1980's, Wilson would frequently ask Spurrier what play he was calling. The extremely confident (and immodest) Spurrier would answer the query about the play selection by saying, "Touchdown, coach." Wilson said that in many instances his coordinator's touchdown prediction was right on the money.

While serving as head ball coach at Duke in the late 1980's, Spurrier called a local sportswriter, and asked that he not be referred to as an "offensive genius" anymore. When the writer asked Spurrier what he preferred to be called, the coach pondered the matter for a moment before saying "I don't know. How about 'mastermind'?"

A *Sporting News* feature on Spurrier in 1994 said that Spurrier's explanations of his huge victory margins could have caused his arrest for "pre-meditated immodesty." Florida quarterback Terry Dean had his share of run-ins with his coach, and when reporters asked the player if he considered Spurrier arrogant, Dean observed, "I don't see him as overly arrogant, maybe egomaniacal."

When Birmingham radio talk show host and *Mobile Register* columnist Paul Finebaum was asked to assess the size of the coach's ego, the sports personality said, "Spurrier has such a large ego that he bows when it thunders."

IV.
POST
GAINESVILLE

25
Poor, Poor Peyton in Indianapolis

AFTER FINISHING HIS CAREER at the University of Tennessee in 1997, Peyton Manning was taken as the No. 1 overall pick by the Indianapolis Colts in the 1998 NFL Draft. The heralded signal caller was a top draft pick in professional football because of his strong and accurate throwing arm, and his uncanny ability to pick a defense apart by calling exactly the right play to counteract the defensive scheme.

Manning, the son of former New Orleans Saints quarterback Archie Manning, did not take long to get into the swing of professional football, and he has started every game for the Colts since he joined the team in 1998. He has made the pro bowl team every year except his rookie season, and led the

NFL in passing yards, completions, and touchdown passes in 2000, which was only his third year in the league.

Steve Spurrier surprised the college football world when he resigned his position as head coach at Florida after the 2001 season. Shortly thereafter Washington Redskins owner Dan Snyder signed the self-proclaimed "Head Ball Coach" to a lucrative long-term contract to restore the Redskins to the championship status they had achieved under former coach Joe Gibbs.

Spurrier's stint back in professional football was nowhere near as successful as it had been at Florida. When Spurrier had his first (and only) encounter with Manning's Colts in the seventh game of the 2002 season, the Redskins had a less than imposing 2-4 record and had stumbled to three consecutive losses. Not only that, the Redskins had lost their previous two games by an average of nearly twenty points. Indianapolis, meanwhile, came into the game with a respectable 4-2 record, and was favored to beat Spurrier's slumping team.

Despite the disparity in records, the Redskins opened the game like they meant business. Washington's first drive ended with a 40-yard field goal to give them a 3-0 lead barely five minutes into the first quarter. On their next possession, Redskins' quarterback Shane Matthews, who had starred for Spurrier at Florida, engineered a drive that culminated in a touchdown pass to give Washington a 10-0 advantage. The Redskins completely dominated the first quarter, controlling the ball for more than eleven minutes as they piled up 140 yards of offense, while holding the Manning-led Colts to only eight yards.

The Redskins continued their domination in the second quarter with an eleven-play, seventy-eight-yard drive that ended with Matthews lofting a thirty-three-yard touchdown pass to stretch their lead to 17-0. Two possessions later a twenty-three-yard field goal gave the Redskins a 20-0 lead with 6:10 left in the first half. After the Redskins lost a fumble on their own four-yard line on their next possession, Manning finally put the Colts on the scoreboard with a one-yard bootleg run for a touchdown. However, Washington responded with a forty-one-yard field goal to extend their lead to 23-7 as time expired at the end of the first half.

After the Redskins were stopped on the Colts' five-yard line midway through the third quarter, Manning led Indianapolis on a fourteen-play, ninety-five-yard touchdown drive, during which he completed eight consecutive passes. After the Colts succeeded on a two-point conversion after the touchdown, they only trailed by 23-15. After forcing a punt on the Redskins' next possession, the Colts were on Washington's forty-yard line after a thirty-yard punt return. The Colts' quarterback needed only five plays to score another touchdown as he ended the drive with a twenty-six-yard pass. However, Manning's pass attempt for the tying two-point conversion was batted away with 6:46 left in the game, leaving the Redskins ahead, 23-21.

Washington then utilized a thirteen-play drive, which ended in a field goal to increase their lead to 26-21, to put the game on ice. Manning finished the game with 214 passing yards by completing twenty-one of thirty-two pass attempts, but his two costly interceptions put the Colts in a hole early in the game.

After the game, as a frustrated Manning discussed his fifth loss to a Spurrier-coached team in five attempts, he said, "This is the National Football League, and you never like to lose to anyone. It doesn't matter who is playing or coaching the other team."

26
Poor Peyton—
A Spoiled Retirement

WHEN PEYTON MANNING FINISHED his career at the University of Tennessee, he was one of the most beloved athletes in the long and proud history of the Volunteers. By the end of his last season in Knoxville (1997), he held forty-two NCAA, Southeastern Conference, and UT records. Following his senior year, he won the Maxwell Award as the nation's outstanding college football player, the Davey O'Brien National Quarterback Award and the Johnny Unitas Golden Arm Award, and he was voted player of the year in the Southeastern Conference. He also won the Sullivan Award as the nation's outstanding amateur athlete.

Although Manning had received many honors during his football career, October 29, 2005 was one of the proudest days in his life, because it was on that day that his famed No. 16 orange jersey was retired by the University of Tennessee during halftime ceremonies at Neyland Stadium. On that day, Peyton was joined in Knoxville for the momentous occasion by his wife, mother, and dad, as well as more than 107,000 UT fans. The fans turned out in large numbers to watch as Peyton participated in the "Vol Walk," where coaches and players walked down Peyton Manning Pass to Neyland Stadium before the game. However, as fate would have it, the opposing team for the Volunteers that day was the University of South Carolina. The first-year coach of the Gamecocks was none other than Peyton's long-time nemesis, one Stephen Orr Spurrier.

Before the 2005 season began, it had not appeared that beating South Carolina would be an especially difficult mission for Tennessee. The Vols were ranked third in the Associated Press preseason poll, while the Gamecocks were facing a season of diminished expectations, partially attributable to NCAA infractions that were uncovered during Lou Holtz's last year as coach at USC. Additionally, the Gamecocks had not beaten Tennessee since 1992, and Coach Phillip Fulmer had never lost to USC. Coach Johnny Majors had been forced out as the Volunteers' coach six days after a 1992 loss to South Carolina.

In the week leading up to the game, Spurrier reminded his players that a victory over Tennessee would be a historic event, since the Gamecocks had never won a game at Neyland Stadium. He observed to the press that during the Florida-Tennessee showdowns of old, the SEC Eastern Division was frequently on the line, but the stakes in his first match with the Vols while leading the Gamecocks were not quite as high.

"Here we are going into our eighth game and they're going into their seventh, and we actually have little bit of a better record than they do. Who would have thunk that?"

However, Spurrier could not resist the temptation to poke some subtle (by Spurrier's standards) fun at Fulmer and the Volunteers. He noted, "What is stranger, I guess, is that before the season began, I think they were picked pretty much by most people to win the Eastern Division, and maybe win the SEC. Here we are going into our eighth game and they're going into their seventh, and we actually have a little bit of a better record than they do. Who would have thunk that?"

When the game began, Spurrier was not wearing his trademark visor. However, not much else was different from the usual outcome when the brash coach visited Neyland Stadium. Carolina quarterback Blake Mitchell completed twenty-two of thirty-six passes for 242 yards, and star receiver Sidney Rice had eight catches for 122 yards, but the outcome of the game was not decided until kicker Josh Brown, who was not known for his long kicks, drilled a forty-nine-yard field goal to give the Gamecocks a historic 16-15 victory that Spurrier labeled a "memory of a lifetime." Brown's kick sent a disappointed Manning home for the sixth consecutive time in head-to-head clashes with "Darth Visor."

27
Potpourri

FORMER AUBURN COACH TERRY BOWDEN said, "On a bad day, Steve Spurrier would just beat you bad; on a good day he would humiliate you."

During his farewell press conference, when he resigned as coach of the Florida Gators, Spurrier could not resist getting in one final jab at Florida State when he said, "I guess that I'm supposed to cry because that's what all those FSU people say I do."

Bobby Bowden commented on Spurrier's brutal honesty by remarking, "He says things that a lot of us think, but don't have guts enough to say." Bowden also described Spurrier as a "piece of work who is the

absolute master of needling you." He declared that
his longtime rival is "going to say or do something
you're not going to like. Let it get under your skin,
and that's what he wants."

Although most college football teams prefer to wear
their dark jerseys in their school colors for home
games, LSU has always preferred to wear their white
jerseys trimmed in purple for their home games in
Baton Rouge. The impish Spurrier, who was always
trying to get a psychological edge on the opposition,
would frequently show up in Tiger Stadium with his
Florida Gators wearing their white road jerseys to
force the Bayou Bengals to wear the dark purple jerseys that they did not like to wear. The sly Gator
coach would blame the mix-up on an equipment
manager who had failed to pack the Gators' dark
blue jerseys for the road game.

After a reporter observed that Georgia had no
chance to beat the Gators in 1997, the Bulldogs
responded by trouncing Florida by a 37-17 score. As
the 1998 game with Georgia approached, Spurrier
implored the reporter to say that Florida had no
chance to beat the Bulldogs.

After beating Tennessee in 1997, Spurrier needled future opponents LSU and Auburn by observing that although those two teams could pose more of a challenge to his Gators than the Volunteers had, the Gators " had had good success in both of those places."

When Spurrier returned to the Southeastern Conference as coach at South Carolina, former Auburn coach Pat Dye said, "He is great for the conference. I like Steve because he is what he is. He's cocky, he's arrogant, and he makes no apologies for it. I respect that."

In 1990 after Florida drubbed Auburn by a 48-7 score, the head Gator added insult to injury by reporting that twenty books had been burned during a dorm fire on the Auburn campus during the game. According to Spurrier, the real tragedy was that "fifteen of the books had not even been colored yet."

One observer described Spurrier's "Emory and Henry" play that featured offensive tackles split fifteen yards from the guards as "eleven guys who got lost on the way to the huddle."

Auburn's Terry Bowden observed, "There are some people it's fun to compete against. Steve's not one of them."

When a reporter queried Spurrier about how it felt to be sixty years old, the Head Ball Coach responded by quoting baseball legend Satchel Paige's question, "How old would you be if you didn't know how old you were?"

Charles Pierce observed in an *Esquire* article, "It isn't easy being the most reviled man in college sports. But Steve Spurrier works at it."

Although Tennessee was ranked third in the nation in the 2005 pre-season Associated Press poll, the Volunteers compiled a less-than-spectacular 5-6 record that year. Two of the losses were to teams that the pre-season prognosticators gave little chance of beating the Volunteers—perennial SEC doormat Vanderbilt and Spurrier's South Carolina Gamecocks. When Spurrier was asked at SEC Media Days prior to the 2006 season what Carolina had done to beat the mighty Volunteers, he replied "I don't know—I guess the same thing Vanderbilt did."

Bibliography

Adams, John, "Let the Game Begin," *The Sporting News*, September 23, 1996.

Associated Press, " 'Evil Genius' Returns to Bedevil Georgia," DesertNews.com, September 7, 2005.

Associated Press, "Spurrier, Fulmer Renew SEC Rivalry," MSNBC.com, October 28, 2005.

Associated Press, "Tennessee to Retire Manning's Number," MSNBC.com, October 28, 2005.

Barnhart, Tony, "Ol' Evil Genius Remains a Blue Chip Quipster," Cox News Service, January 29, 2006.

Barnhart, Tony, "Payback Awaits SEC Agitator," Cox News Service, September 1, 2005.

Basilio, Tony, "Love to Hate—Spurrier's Gators Were the Vols' Favorite Enemy," *Metro Pulse*, September 9, 2004.

Biddle, Joe, "SEC Experiencing Meltdown of Offenses," *The Tennessean*, September 23, 2005.

Bisher, Furman, "Admit It: It's Nice to Have Spurrier Back," *The Atlanta Journal-Constitution*, September 6, 2005.

Bowles, Jerry. *A Thousand Sundays—The Story of the Ed Sullivan Show*. New York: G. P. Putnam's Sons, 1980.

Celebrity Anecdotes. Anecdotage.com.

Chastain, Bill. *The Steve Spurrier Story—From Heisman to Head Ball Coach*, Dallas: Taylor Trade Publishing, 2002.

Clayton, Ward, "We Want Mail, So Here's Some Fodder to Spurrier You On," *Augusta Chronicle*, January 4, 1997.

Davis, Elizabeth A., "Fulmer Jabs at Spurrier for His Remark About Tennessee Arrests," *The Maryville Tennessee Daily Times*, April 15, 2005.

Davis, Elizabeth A., "Tennessee Retires Manning's Number," comcast.net, October 29, 2005.

Dent, Jim, "Spurrier's Wit Stirred the Gators-Vols Rivalry," ESPN.com, September 20, 2002.

Drehs, Wayne, "I Would Like to Whip Him and He Would Like to Whip Me," ESPN.com, November 17, 20000.

Duffey, Gene, "Tide's Freshman Guard Draws Ire of Florida Coach After Jilting Gators," *Huntsville Times*, August 7, 2000.

Elliott, Jeff, "Resignation Shocks Broadcasters," Morris News Service, January 7, 2002.

Fowler, Chris, "Can't Get Used to Mediocre 'Noles—Neither Can Gators," ESPN.com, November 15, 2001.

Frias, Carlos, "Tigers Missed the Mark By Picking Archer," alligator.org, Fall 1996.

"Greatest Cocktail Parties of the Past," uga.rivals.com, October 26, 2004.

Hayes, Mark, "Lowly Gamecocks Have Visored Visions of Glory," *The Sporting News*, February 7, 2005.

Hillyard, Jonathan, "SEC Legends Renew Old Rivalry in Knoxville," The Daily Gamecock Online, October 28, 2005.

Hunt, Ryan, "Gators Crush 'Cats Again, 65-0," Alligator.org, Fall 1996.

Johnston, Joey, "Compelling Figure: Steve Spurrier," *The Tampa Tribune*, November 22, 2005.

Johnston, Joey, "You Know What FSU Stands for, Don't You? Free Shoes University," *The Tampa Tribune*, November 25, 2005.

Kendall, Josh, "Decision Shocks Dooley," *Athens Banner-Herald*, January 5, 2002.

Kindred, Dave, "Spurrier Dares to Imagine—Always," *The Sporting News*, January 28, 2002.

Kindred, Dave, "The Spurrier Syndrome," *The Sporting News*, September 22, 1997.

Kindred, Dave, "Unconventional Wisdom—Florida Gators Coach Steve Spurrier," *The Sporting News*, December 12, 1994.

Layden, Tim, "Putting Peyton in His Place," *Sports Illustrated*, September 22, 1997.

LoCicero, Geoff, "The Three Faces of Steve," *Carolinian*, August 1, 2005.

Looney, Douglas S., "The Great Offender—Florida Football Coach Steve Spurrier," *The Sporting News*, November 20, 1995.

Low, Chris, "Spurrier Rekindles Painful Memories," *The Tennessean*, October 29, 2005.

Mizell, Hubert, "Look for Spurrier in Center of Storm," *St. Petersburg Times*, September 24, 2000.

Morris, Ron, "The Life and Times of Steve Spurrier," dcgators.com, November 24, 2004.

Neiswanger, Robbie, "The Ol' Ball Coach Returns to the SEC," The Morning News/Razorback Central, July 28, 2005.

Pells, Eddie, "Spurrier Goes Out Laughing," *Athens Banner-Herald*, January 8, 2002.

Pierce, Charles, "The Little Emperor," *Esquire*, January 1, 2001.

Price, S. L., "Steve Superior," *Sports Illustrated*, October 25, 1995.

Bibliography

Rosenblatt, Richard, "Florida Spoils Manning's Day in 33-20 Win Over Tennessee," *SouthCoast Today*, September 18, 1997.

Schlabach, Mark, "After NFL, Spurrier Realizes Pros of College Ball," *Washington Post*, September 1, 2005.

Schlabach, Mark, "Spurrier Is Back—Let the Fun Begin," *Washington Post*, July 28, 2005.

Shepherd, David, "Mirror Images 1990 vs. 2005," GatorCountry.com, July 19, 2005.

Sports Illustrated.com, October 28, 2002.

Spurrier Press Conference Transcription, January 7, 2002, gatorzone.com.

Stone, Christian, "Line of the Week," *Sports Illustrated*, September 11, 1995.

Strelow, Paul, "New Coach Shelves His Swagger—For Now," *Spartanburg Herald-Journal*, November 24, 2004.

Sumner, Jim, "Jim Sumner on Duke/UNC Gridiron History," *Duke Basketball Report*, November 15, 2000.

Szulszteyn, Andrea, "This Time, UF Could Lose to Bulldogs—Or Not," Alligator Online, Fall 1998.

Torgerson, Stan, "Steve Spurrier Can Walk the Walk and Talk the Talk," *The Daily Mississippian*, October 1, 1997.

Weber, Rick, "Ball Coach Won't Be Short on Zingers," Trailer-bodybuilders.com, January 1, 2003.

Wetzel, Dan, "The Ol' Ball Coach Is Back," Yahoo Sports, April 19, 2005.

Whiteside, Kelly, "Tigers Stroll Down Memory Lane," *USA Today*, January 1, 2004.

Zemek, Matthew, "Why Steve Spurrier Matters," *College Football News*, November 10, 2004.

Zenor, John, "Not All SEC Coaches Glad to See Spurrier Go," secsports.com, August 4, 2002.

Zillgitt, Jeff, "New League, New World for Spurrier," *USA Today*, November 21, 2002.

Notes

1.   Alone Behind Enemy Lines. Joe Biddle interview.

2.   Two for One Recruiting. Biddle interview. Ken Lyon interview.

3.   The Next Great Quarterback. Biddle interview. Graham Spurrier interview. Lyon interview.

4.   Steve the Scholar. Bill Chastain, *The Steve Spurrier Story – From Heisman to Head Ball Coach*, p. 63. Douglas S. Looney, "The Great Offender – Florida Football Coach Steve Spurrier." Biddle interview. Spurrier interview.

5.   Right Here on Our Stage. Jerry Bowles, *A Thousand Sundays – The Story of the Ed Sullivan Show*, p. 174. Chastain, p. 63.

6.   Coach, Your Son Stinks. Chastain, pp. 90-91. Biddle interview.

7.   Right Here in Tampa. Celebrity Anecdotes. Biddle interview. Letter from Steve Spurrier.

8.   Knifing the Mack. Jim Sumner, Jim Sumner on Duke/UNC Gridiron History. Ward Clayton, "We Want Mail, So Here's Some Fodder to Spurrier You On." Biddle interview.

9.   Low-Stress Recruiting. Biddle interview.

10.   The One That Got Away. Carlos Frias, "Tigers Missed the Mark by Picking Archer." Kelly Whiteside, "Tigers Stroll Down Memory Lane."

11.   Settling An Old Score. S. L. Price, "Steve Superior." Looney. Ryan Hunt, "Gators Crush' Cats Again, 65-0." Matt Hayes, "Lowly Gamecocks Have Visored Visions of Glory." Biddle interview.

12.   The Tweaking of the Orange. Dan Wetzel, "The Ol' Ball Coach is Back." Elizabeth A. Davis, "Fulmer Jabs at Spurrier for His Remark about Tennessee Arrests." Dave Kindred, "The Spurrier Syndrome." Tim Layden, "Putting Peyton in His Place." Chris Low, "Spurrier Rekindles Painful Memories." Stan Torgerson, "Steve Spurrier Can Walk the Walk and Talk the Talk." Biddle interview.

13.   Revenge Against the Bulldogs. Associated Press, "' Evil Genius' Returns to Bedevil Georgia." Looney. "Greatest Cocktail Parties of the Past." David Shepherd, "Mirror Images 1990 vs. 2005." Jeff Elliott, "Resignation Shocks Broadcasters."

14.   A Sideshow on the Sideline. Matthew Zemek, "Why Steve Spurrier Matters." Eddie Pells , "Spurrier Goes Out Laughing." Spurrier Press Conference Transcription.

15.   Poor, Poor Peyton. Torgerson. Layden. Richard Rosenblatt, "Florida Spoils Manning's Day in 33-20 Win Over Tennessee."

16.   Me and Phil. Jonathan Hillyard, "SEC Legends Renew Old Rivalry in Knoxville." John Adams, "Let the Game Begin." Associated Press, "Spurrier, Fulmer Renew SEC Rivalry." Jim Dent, "Spurrier's Wit Stirred the Gators-Vols Rivalry." Robbie Neiswanger, "The Ol' Ball Coach returns to the SEC." Mark Schlabach, "Spurrier Is Back — Let the Fun Begin." John Zenor, "Not All SEC Coaches Glad to See Spurrier Go." Biddle interview.

17. Where Have All the Blue Chippers Gone? Tony Barnhart, "Ol' Evil Genius Remains A Blue Chip Quipster." Wetzel. Price. Mark Schlabach, "After NFL, Spurrier Realizes Pros of College Ball." Biddle interview.

18. Free Shoes University. Joey Johnston, "You Know What FSU stands for, Don't You? Free Shoes University." Price. Looney. Joey Johnston, "Compelling Figure: Steve Spurrier."

19. Darth Visor. Joe Biddle, "SEC Experiencing Meltdown of Offenses." Looney. Joey Johnston, "Compelling Figure: Steve Spurrier.' Biddle interview.

20. Ruffians in Tallahassee. Joey Johnston, "Compelling Figure: Steve Spurrier." Zemek. Dave Kindred, "Spurrier Dares to Imagine—Always." Rick Weber, "Ball Coach Won't Be Short on Zingers."

21. It's Hard to Be Humble. Looney. Weber. Paul Strelow, "New Coach Shelves His Swagger—For Now." Zenor. Geoff LoCicero, "The Three Faces of Steve." Biddle interview.

22. Love Me, Love My Dog. Gene Duffey, "Tide's Freshman Guard Draws Ire of Florida Coach After Jilting Gators. Paul Gattis letter.

23. You Can't Score Too Many. Jeff Zillgitt, "New League, New World for Spurrier." Chris Fowler, "Can't Get Used to Mediocre 'Noles – Neither Can the Gators." Price. Adams. Looney. Hubert Mizell, "Look for Spurrier in Center of Storm." Josh Kendall, "Decision Shocks Dooley." Christian Stone, "Line of the Week."

24. Modesty Has Its Place. Price. Shepherd. Kindred, "Spurrier Dares to Imagine – Always." Looney. Biddle interview.

25. Poor, Poor Peyton in Indianapolis. Sports Illustrated.com, October 28, 2002. Huntsville Times, October 28, 2002.

26. Poor Peyton, A Spoiled Retirement. Associated Press, "Tennessee to Retire Manning's Number." Elizabeth A. Davis, "Tennessee Retires Manning's Number." Low.

27. Potpourri. Andrea Szulszteyn, "This Time Florida Could Lose to Bulldogs – Or Not." Torgerson. Tony Barnhart, "Payback Awaits SEC Agitator." Davis, "Tennessee Retires Manning's Number." Kindred, "Spurrier Dares to Imagine – Always." Charles Pierce, "The Little Emperor." Pells. Biddle interview.

Author

Author Richard Sikes, a resident of Huntsville, Alabama, is a manufacturing financial executive and part-time historian. This is his second book. His first book was *Laughing With the Bear: Humorous Tales of a Coaching Legend*.